CODE
BREAKER

CODE
BREAKER

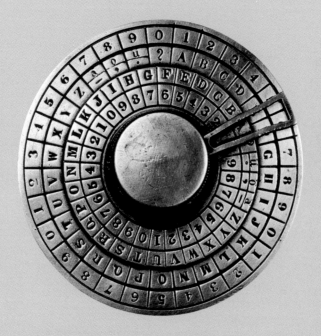

THE HISTORY OF
SECRET COMMUNICATION

Stephen Pincock & Mark Frary

rh
BOOKS

Published by Random House Books in 2007

Conceived and produced by
Elwin Street Limited
Third floor, 144 Liverpool Road
London N1 1LA
www.elwinstreet.com

Illustration: Richard Burgess
Page design: Counterpunch/Peter Ross
Jacket design: Juliet Rowley

A CIP catalogue record for this book is available from the British Library.

ISBN: 978-1-905-21154-8

10 9 8 7 6 5 4 3 2 1

Printed in Singapore

CONTENTS

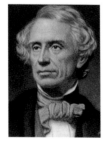

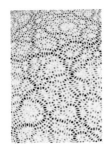

INTRODUCTION

In the modern world, the very air around us hums with encryption. Every call we make on a mobile phone, every cable television channel we watch, each time we withdraw cash from an ATM, we rely on sophisticated forms of computer encryption to ensure the prying ears and eyes of others are excluded. But modern times have no monopoly on secrecy. Over the past 2,000 years or more, codes and ciphers have played vital, sometimes defining, roles in politics, the bloody theatre of war, assassination and the fight against crime. Wars have been won and lost, empires built or destroyed and individual lives raised up or ruined by messages passed in secret. With so much at stake, it comes as no surprise that a never-ending battle rages between cryptographers – those who strive to hide the meaning of a message behind a code or cipher – and cryptanalysts, the resourceful and cunning codebreakers whose avowed goal is to crack those codes and ciphers to reveal what lies behind them.

Each time cryptographers invent a new code or cipher, the cryptanalysts are thrown into the dark. Coded messages that were easily cracked hitherto are suddenly impenetrable. But the battle is never over. With dogged perseverance, or an illuminating flash of inspiration, the cryptanalysts eventually find a chink in the armour, working at it tirelessly until the secret messages reveal themselves once more.

The remarkable men and women who have entered the trade of the cryptanalyst have revealed a series of traits that suit them to their difficult and often dangerous work. For a start, they often exhibit startling originality of thought. One of the greatest cryptanalysts in history, Alan Turing, whose work helped turn the tide of the Second World War, was among the most original thinkers of his time.

Successful cryptanalysts are also defined by their level of motivation. Nothing captivates the human mind like secrets, and for some codebreakers the struggle to unravel them is often motivation enough. Yet, there are other motivators – patriotism, revenge, greed or a desire for greater knowledge.

Unravelling codes and ciphers takes more than a passing interest. Although the early alphabetic shift cipher favoured by Julius Caesar now seems childishly simple to crack, Caesar's enemies at the time needed to persevere to unlock his coded messages. Indeed, it is often because the vast majority of would-be codebreakers do not persevere that codes remain unbroken.

Speed is also of the essence in codebreaking. Many codes and ciphers are breakable – but only if one has enough time to work on them. The RSA cipher is a classic example. It relies on the quirk that multiplying two prime numbers together takes only a little time, but trying to find out which prime numbers have been multiplied to achieve a given number can take forever, even using a computer.

Codebreakers also need vision. They often work under a shroud of official or criminal secrecy, and frequently the sensitive nature of what they do requires them to work alone. Without a vision of the final goal, the cryptanalyst works in vain.

This book shows how the tide of history has often turned on the codes that have been made and broken. It is little wonder that they have a strong grip on our imagination, and explains the success of code-riddled novels like *The Da Vinci Code* and the regular appearance of codebreakers on television and in the movies.

While the real world does not exactly resemble those fictional settings, the true history of cryptology – and cryptanalysis in particular – is, if anything, stranger than anything a thriller writer could dream up. In the following pages, you will discover just how extraordinary the people who become codebreakers actually are. You will meet some of the most intriguing people in history and find out the fundamental skills that make up the weaponry of the codebreaker.

But that's not all. Throughout the book, we give you the chance to use those crucial tools yourself. We have crafted seven cunning codes that draw on the lessons learned in each chapter, and want you to tackle them. Cracking them will be hard – you will certainly need originality of thought, good fortune, perseverance and vision.

CHAPTER ONE

ORIGINALITY

From ancient Egypt to Mary Queen of Scots,
via the codes of sex and religion.
Simple substitutions, transpositions and frequency analysis.

It's hard to imagine a human society existing without secrets – existing without intrigue, plots, political backstabbing, warfare, commercial gain or love affairs. It should come as no surprise, therefore, that the history of covert messages and secret writing stretches back to some of the world's most ancient civilisations.

The roots of cryptography can be traced back nearly 4,000 years to ancient Egypt, when scribes carving histories into the rock of great monuments began subtly to alter the use and purpose of the hieroglyphics they carved.

The aim of their contrivances probably wasn't to conceal the meaning of their words; instead, they may have wanted to bemuse or entertain passing readers, or perhaps to increase the mystery and magic of religious texts. But in doing so, they foreshadowed the real cryptography that evolved over the following millennia.

The Egyptians were not alone in developing means of secret writing. In Mesopotamia, for example, the techniques were taken into other walks of life, as illustrated by a tiny tablet found at the site of Seleucia, about 30 kilometres (18 miles) from modern-day Baghdad on the banks of the Tigris River. The pocket-sized tablet, dated to around 1500 BCE, bears an encrypted formula for making pottery

Opposite: The roots of cryptography can be seen in Egyptian hieroglyphics.

glazes. Whoever wrote the instructions used cuneiform signs in their least common syllabic values – unusual groups of consonants and vowels – as a way to guard his valuable trade secret.

The Babylonians, the Assyrians and the Greeks also developed their own means of hiding the meaning of their messages. And in the time of the Romans came the first major historical figure whose name has become permanently attached to a cryptographic method: Julius Caesar.

CAESAR'S SECRET WRITING

Caesar is remembered as the most famous ruler of ancient Rome. As a general, he was renowned for his daring; as a politician, he overwhelmed his enemies with clear-sighted brilliance; and as a man, he combined a flamboyant fashion sense and rampant sex drive with a gambler's willingness to risk it all. He was smart, daring and ruthless – all of which are excellent characteristics for a successful codemaker to possess.

Above: Gaius Julius Caesar (100 BCE to 44 BCE), famed Roman military and political leader, devised and implemented the early Caesar shift cipher.

In his military memoir, the *Gallic Wars*, Caesar described how he cunningly obscured the meaning of a vital wartime message in case the enemy intercepted it.

During the Romans' campaign against local armies in the regions we now know as modern-day France, Belgium and Switzerland, Caesar's officer Cicero was besieged, and nearing surrender. Caesar wanted to let him know help was at hand without tipping off the enemy, so he sent a messenger bearing a letter written in Latin, but using Greek letters. The messenger was told that if he couldn't enter Cicero's camp, he should throw his spear inside the fortification with the letter fastened to the thong.

'The Gaul discharged the spear as he had been instructed,' Caesar recalled. 'By chance it stuck fast in the tower and for two days was not sighted by our troops; on the third day it was sighted by a soldier, taken down and delivered to Cicero. He read it through and then recited it at a parade of the troops, bringing the greatest rejoicing to all.'

Caesar's use of secret writing was familiar to the ancients. The historian Suetonius Tranquillus, describing his life more than 100 years later, wrote that if Caesar ever had anything confidential he needed to say, 'he wrote it in cipher'.

THE DEFINING QUALITIES OF CIPHERS AND CODES

Tranquillus' use of the word 'cipher' is worth noting because, although we tend to use it interchangeably with the word 'code', there are actually some important differences between them.

In essence, the distinction is as follows: **ciphers** are systems for disguising the meaning of a message by replacing each of the individual letters in the message with other symbols. **Codes**, on the other hand, place more emphasis on meanings than characters, and tend to replace whole words or phrases according to a list contained in a code-book.

Another difference between codes and ciphers relates to their level of inbuilt flexibility. Codes are static, relying on the set of words and phrases in a code-book to conceal the meaning of a message.

For example, a code might specify that the group of numbers '5487' replaces the word 'attack'. This means that any time 'attack' is written in a message, the encoded version will include the **code group** '5487'. Even if a code-book includes several options for encoding 'attack', the number of variations will be limited.

In contrast, ciphers tend to be inherently more flexible, and the way a word like 'attack' is enciphered might depend on its position in the message and a host of other variables that are defined by the rules of the cipher system. This means that the same letter, word or phrase in a message could be encrypted in completely different ways in different parts of the same message.

For any cipher system, the general rules used to encrypt a message are referred to as the **algorithm**. The **key** specifies the exact details of the encryption on any particular occasion.

HIDDEN WRITING

As well as being adept at cryptography, the Greeks used another form of secret writing, known as **steganography**. While cryptography aims to disguise the meaning of a message, steganography is supposed to hide the fact that there's a message at all.

Herodotus, sometimes called the father of history, described several examples of this in his *Histories*. In one episode, he told of a noble man called Harpagus who sought revenge on the king of the Medes, who had previously tricked him into eating his own son. Harpagus hid a message to a potential ally inside a dead hare and sent a messenger disguised as a hunter to deliver it. The message got through, the alliance was formed and, eventually, the king of the Medes was overthrown.

The Greeks also hid messages under the wax of wax tablets as a way of avoiding their detection.

Another, more gruesome, method involved tattooing messages into the shaved scalp of slaves. Once the unfortunate messenger's hair had grown back, and assuming he didn't die of blood poisoning in the meantime, he would be sent on his way to deliver the message in person. At his destination, the messenger's head would be shaved again by the intended recipient, who could read the message at his leisure.

Using shaved slaves to deliver messages in secret clearly has its downsides. It must have been a slow process, for one thing. But steganography has survived into the modern era where it has been much loved by spies. In fact, there are a multitude of different steganographic methods just as there are cryptographic. These range from the use of invisible inks by spies throughout the ages to cunning modern-day technological techniques for secreting data within digital images or music files.

Above: Herodotus of Halicarnassus, the fifth-century BCE scholar and historian, refers to early instances of steganography in his *Histories*.

The Greeks seem to have been experts at secret writing. The historian Polybius, for example, came up with a system whose use extended into modern times (see page 16).

Polybius' 'checkerboard' method, as it's called, may have been used by the Greeks to signal via flaming torches – for example holding two torches in the left hand and one in the right would signal the letter 'b' – and it was later used as the basis for more complicated ciphers.

Perhaps as far back as the seventh century BCE, the warlike Spartans were known to use a device known as a scytale to carry secret messages using a kind of transposition cipher.

The Greek historian Plutarch described how it worked:

'When the [rulers] send out an admiral or a general, they make two round pieces of wood exactly alike in length and thickness, so that each corresponds to the other in its dimensions, and keep one themselves, while they give the other to their envoy. These pieces of wood they call scytalae. Whenever, then, they wish to send some secret and important message, they make a scroll of parchment long and narrow, like a leather strap, and wind it round their scytale, leaving no vacant space thereon, but covering its surface all round with the parchment. After doing this, they write what they wish on the parchment, just as it lies wrapped about the scytale; and when they have written their message, they take the parchment off and send it, without the piece of wood, to the commander. He, when he has received it, cannot otherwise get any meaning out of it – since the letters have no connection, but are disarranged – unless he takes his own scytale and winds the strip of parchment about it.'

Above: Mestrius Plutarchus (Plutarch) (c. 46–127 CE), Greek historian, biographer and essayist who detailed the workings of the scytale.

Above: Could the enciphered messages of the scytale have led the Spartans to victory? Spartan Pausanias leads his army to defeat a Persian army twice its size.

SECRET WRITING

Polybius arranged the letters of the alphabet in a 5 x 5 grid (with i and j sharing a cell), and assigned numbers from 1 to 5 for each of the columns and rows.

	1	2	3	4	5
1	a	b	c	d	e
2	f	g	h	i/j	k
3	l	m	n	o	p
4	q	r	s	t	u
5	v	w	x	y	z

This allows each letter to be represented by two numbers. The letter **c** is 13, for example, while **m** is 32.

UNDERSTANDING THE CAESAR SHIFT

By the time Suetonius was writing about Julius Caesar, the secrets of his ciphers were well known. Anyone who wanted to decipher his letters and get at their meaning, Suetonius wrote, 'must substitute the fourth letter of the alphabet, namely D, for A, and so with the others'.

Plain	a b c d e f g h i j k l m n o p q r s t u v w x y z
Cipher	D E F G H I J K L M N O P Q R S T U V W X Y Z A B C

This type of cipher is known as a **Caesar shift**. According to Suetonius, Caesar kept his secrets hidden by shifting the letters just three places to the left. But the same principle applies if you shift the letters anywhere from one to 25 places. For letters further into the alphabet, if the shift moves them beyond Z, the alphabet 'wraps around' – so the letter y shifted three places becomes B.

For example, if you wanted to write Caesar's famous statement 'veni, vidi, vici' (I came, I saw, I conquered) using his cipher, the result would be YHQL, YLGL, YLFL.

DECIPHERING CAESAR

Cracking a message written using a Caesar shift cipher is relatively easy because there are only a limited number of possible shifts – just 25 in English.

Take the following brief enciphered message, for example:

FIAEVI XLI MHIW SJ QEVGL

The most straightforward approach to deciphering this is to write out a short segment of the ciphertext in a table, and below it write out all the different possible shifts that might have been performed. Sometimes this technique is referred to as 'completing the plain component'.

You only need to keep writing out the different alphabets until you get one that makes sense.

Number of letters shifted	Possible plaintext
0	FIAEVI XLI
1	EHZDUH WKH
2	DGYCTG VJG
3	CFXBSF UIF
4	BEWARE THE

The appearance of sensible words at this point suggests that the alphabet has been shifted four letters to make the encipherment. Deciphering the remainder shows that the message is 'Beware the Ides of March'.

Plain	a	b	c	d	e	f	g	h	i	j	k	l	m	n	o	p	q	r	s	t	u	v	w	x	y	z
Cipher	E	F	G	H	I	J	K	L	M	N	O	P	Q	R	S	T	U	V	W	X	Y	Z	A	B	C	D

One way to speed up the process of deciphering Caesar shifts is to prepare a series of strips of paper on which you've written the alphabet in reverse order. If you align the strips so that they make up the ciphertext along one of their rows, then it is a simple matter to scan down the different rows to find the one that reveals the message.

Ciphers such as Caesar's, where the letters in a message are replaced by another set of letters, are known as **substitution ciphers**. The other broad category of cipher is the **transposition cipher**, in which the letters of a message are shuffled around.

Transpositions can also be achieved using a grid. To take a simple example, someone wanting to send the message 'the ship will sail at dawn heading due east' could write it in rows of five letters and then read the letters down the column to encrypt them.

t	h	e	s	h
i	p	w	i	l
l	s	a	i	l
a	t	d	a	w
n	h	e	a	d
i	n	g	d	u
e	e	a	s	t

This gives the encrypted message:

TILANIEHPSTHNEEWADEGASIIAADSHLLWDUT

CRACKING TRANSPOSITIONS

A good way to approach the deciphering of a message that is known to be a transposition cipher is known as 'anagramming'. This technique involves sliding pieces of ciphertext around and looking for sections that look like anagrams of real words.

A specific technique is called 'multiple anagramming' a strategy that uses the anagram technique on two different ciphertexts in parallel, using each one as a cross-check for the other.

For multiple anagramming to work, you need to have two transpositions that contain the same number of words or letters, and that have been shuffled using the same technique. For a codebreaker monitoring the communications of an enemy over a long enough period of time – perhaps during a war – this may become more likely than it seems at first.

To illustrate how it works, let's take a simple example. Suppose we have two transpositions consisting of five letters each, as follows:

EKSLA
LGEBU

It's fairly apparent that both of these letter groups could be shuffled around to form a couple of different words:

ESKLA could be either LAKES or LEAKS
LEGBU could be either BUGLE or BULGE

If we only had one of the pieces of text, it might not be clear which of the two possibilities is correct. But if we try performing the same unscrambling on both messages in parallel, it becomes clear that only one gives a sensible answer for both messages:

12345	41532	45132	45312
ESKLA	LEAKS	LAEKS	LAKES
LEGBU	BLUGE	BULGE	BUGLE

THE PHAISTOS DISC

Above: The site of the Minoan palace in Crete where the Phaistos Disc was found.

In the early days of July, 1908, a young Italian archaeologist by the name of Luigi Pernier was excavating the Minoan palace site of Phaistos, on the south coast of Crete.

In the heat of the summer, Pernier was working on the main cell of an underground temple depository when he uncovered a remarkably intact chalk-encrusted terracotta disc, about 15 cm (6 inches) across and just over 1 cm (½ inch) thick.

On both sides, the disc was covered with a total of 241 mysterious hieroglyphic stamps, spiralling from the outer rim into the centre. Among the 45 different glyphs – carved or engraved symbolic figures – several obviously represented every-day things, such as people, fish, insects, birds, a boat and so on.

These symbols might be easily recognisable, but what they mean has baffled archaeologists and cryptologists alike in the century that has passed since the disc was found.

A major problem is that no other relics bearing the same type of stamped writings have ever been found, leaving would-be decipherers with only 241 characters to work with.

What makes this paucity all the more frustrating is that on the other side of Crete, at the site of the Minoan palace of Knossos, archaeologists had discovered a hoard of hundreds of tablets written in ancient scripts known as Linear A and Linear B.

While the earlier script, Linear A, remains undeciphered – and in fact is another of the holy grails of ancient scripts – Linear B, which dates from the fourteenth and thirteenth centuries BCE, was cracked in the 1950s when the English architect Michael Bentris discovered the tablets were written in a form of Greek.

Sadly for those fascinated by the Phaistos Disc, many experts think it simply doesn't contain enough script to allow a definitive decipherment. That hasn't stopped scores of people taking a stab at it, however.

Some amateur archaeologists suggest it may be a kind of prayer, others suggest it is a calendar and others still, a call to arms. There have even been proposals that it is an ancient board game or a geometric theorem.

Above: The two sides of the Phaistos Disc. The meaning of the markings, and even where it was made, remain disputed, and make it one of the most famous mysteries of archaeology and cryptology.

One man who has long been interested in the secrets of the Disc is Anthony Svoronos, a mathematician from Crete who now runs a website listing all the various proposed solutions.

'The most important aspect of the Disc – in my opinion – is the technique used to create it,' Svoronos explains. 'The Disc is printed using multiple seals. The effort involved in the construction of those seals was important and as a result we should assume that they were used to produce many different documents. And yet the Disc is the unique document produced with this set of seals that has survived to our days.'

Another interesting point is that the signs stamped upon it are highly detailed and very clear, in contrast to the much more abstract shapes and signs of the Linear scripts.

'Only wild speculations can be used to reconcile these characteristics,' he says. 'My favourite explanation is that the text on the Phaistos Disc is a question placed to an oracle,

and that the ritual at this oracle required that the object inscribed with the question was destroyed during the process of divination.' This theory might explain why, even though many texts were produced, all were destroyed.

'Of course, this is a far fetched interpretation of the events that took place in Phaistos and resulted in the creation of this unique object,' Svoronos admits, but he also notes that there are other pieces of evidence from the area that give it a certain credibility.

On the island of Keros, for example, there is archaeological evidence of a cult predating the Phaistos Disc in which valuable ritual statues were deliberately smashed. And in the oracle of Dodoni, which is very old and possibly predates the Phaistos Disc, there are lead tablets that contain queries to the oracle.

Perhaps this interpretation is the right one, or perhaps it isn't. Either way, the world awaits a definitive explanation for this mysterious artifact.

THE BIRTH OF CODEBREAKING

For thousands of years, the development of cryptography had not been accompanied in any significant way by a similar development in the cipher-cracking techniques of **cryptanalysis**. Those skills were invented among the Arab peoples.

The scholars of Islamic culture's golden age after 750 CE were skilled in the sciences, mathematics, arts and literature. Dictionaries, encyclopaedias and text books of cryptography were published, and the scholarly examination of word origins and sentence structure led to the first major breakthrough in cryptanalysis.

Muslim scholars came to the realisation that letters in any language appear with a regular and reliable frequency. They also came to understand that knowledge of this frequency could be employed to crack ciphers, a technique known as **frequency analysis**.

The first known recorded explanation of cryptanalysis was given by ninth-century Arabic scientist and prolific author, Abu Yusuf Yaqub ibn Ishaq al-Sabbah Al-Kindi, in his work *A Manuscript on Deciphering Cryptographic Messages*.

Opposite: The Islamic Golden Age, which lasted from around 750 CE until the thirteenth century, saw great achievements made by scientists, artists and philosophers – and also the great cryptanalyst Al-Kindi.

Left: A page from Al-Kindi's *A Manuscript on Deciphering Cryptographic Messages*.

FIRST, KNOW YOUR LANGUAGE

Frequency analysis is probably the most fundamental tool required by a codebreaker. Although the precise frequency with which each letter of an alphabet appears will vary from one piece of text to another, there are some regular patterns that are very useful when unravelling a message written in cipher.

For example, in English the letter **e** occurs most often – on average, 12 per cent of the letters in any given piece of writing will be **e**. The next most common are **t, a, o, i, n** and **s**. The least common are **j, q, z** and **x**.

Expected relative frequencies of letters in an English text

Letter	Percentage	Letter	Percentage
A	8.0	N	7.1
B	1.5	O	7.6
C	3.0	P	2.0
D	3.9	Q	0.1
E	12.5	R	6.1
F	2.3	S	6.5
G	1.9	T	9.2
H	5.5	U	2.7
I	7.2	V	1.0
J	0.1	W	1.9
K	0.7	X	0.2
L	4.1	Y	1.7
M	2.5	Z	0.1

(Based on letter counts conducted by Meyer-Matyas and published in *Decrypted Secrets: Methods and Maxims of Cryptography*).

In graph form, this distribution looks something like this:

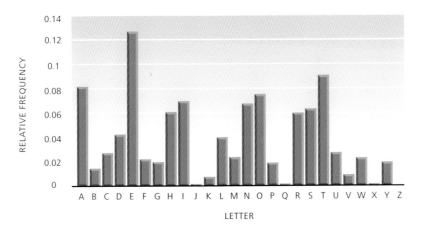

Using this knowledge, you can start by tallying up the frequencies of letters or symbols in an enciphered message and comparing them to the usual frequencies in plaintext.

Next, you need to look at how the letters group together. For example, 'the' is the most frequent three-letter group (**trigraph**) or word in English – and q is usually followed by u. More often than not, n will be preceded by a vowel. Similarly, the pronoun I and the article a are the most common single-letter words.

There is no guarantee that any given text will correspond exactly to the expected frequencies – a scientific paper, for example, will contain a vastly different selection of words to a love letter.

Still, using these crucial fragments of knowledge, cryptanalysts can begin to make correlations between the ciphertext and plaintext and sketch an outline of what some of the letters in the message might be.

With a combination of trial-and-error, perseverance, careful guesswork and luck, it is possible to fill in the blanks and crack the code.

MEDIEVAL CRYPTOGRAPHY

While the Arab world was scaling intellectual heights, in Europe cryptological scholarship was less widely practised. Secret writing during the early medieval period was largely limited to monasteries, where monks would study Biblical and Hebrew ciphers such as the **Atbash cipher**.

One rare example of a cipher being used outside the religious setting during this period has been found in a scientific treatise on the construction and use of an astronomical instrument, called *The Equatorie of the Planetis*. This text, attributed by some scholars to Geoffrey Chaucer (this is queried by others), includes a number of short passages written in cipher, in which the letters of the alphabet were replaced with symbols.

For roughly four centuries after 1400, the dominant method of secret writing was a combination of code and cipher known as a **nomenclator**.

Nomenclators had evolved in southern Europe in the late fourteenth century – a time when wealthy city states such as Venice, Naples and Florence were vying for trading supremacy, while at the same time the Roman Catholic Church had been divided by the disputed claims of two Popes.

Combining the techniques of writing in code and of writing in cipher, nomenclators use a substitution cipher to scramble the text of most of a message while replacing certain words or names by code words or symbols.

For example, a nomenclator might consist of a list of symbols to be substituted for the letters of the alphabet, plus a list of other symbols to be directly substituted for common words or names. So the word 'and' might be written as '2' while 'King of England' becomes '&'.

In the early days, nomenclators would replace a small number of code words with short, one- and two-letter, code equivalents. This would be integrated with a monoalphabetic substitution cipher to muddle the rest of the message. By the eighteenth century their size had grown enormously, and nomenclators used in Russia included code equivalents for thousands of words or syllables.

Above: Illustration of Geoffrey Chaucer, who some believe wrote one of the earliest secular ciphers in medieval Europe.

Opposite: Early map of Venice as a major trading centre in the fourteenth century.

HOLY CODES

Above: A Torah scroll containing the five books of the Old Testament written on goat's skin parchment.

Atbash cipher. Atbash is a traditional Hebrew substitution cipher where the first letter of the Hebrew alphabet is replaced with the last, the second with the second-to-last, and so on. The name derives from the letters alef, tav, bet and shin, the first, last, second and second-to-last letters of the alphabet.

The Atbash Cipher

Alef	Tav
Bet	Shin
Gimel	Resh
Dalet	Qof
He	Tsadi
Vav	Final Tsadi
Zayin	Pe
Het	Final Pe
Tet	Ayin
Yod	Samekh
Final Kaf	Nun
Kaf	Final Nun
Lamed	Mem
Final Mem	Final Mem
Mem	Lamed
Final Nun	Kaf
Nun	Final Kaf
Samekh	Yod
Ayin	Tet
Final Pe	Het
Pe	Zayin
Final Tsadi	Vav
Tsadi	He
Qof	Dalet
Resh	Gimel
Shin	Bet
Tav	Alef

The heady combination of cryptography and religious writing has an unmatched fascination for many people. Nowhere is that better illustrated than in the enormous success of Dan Brown's best-selling fictional work *The Da Vinci Code*, which mixes hidden messages, codes and deep secrets about Christianity into the format of a thriller.

Outside the realms of fiction and fantasy, however, secret writing and religion do have a long shared history, in part out of necessity – persecution can lead religions underground.

Probably the most famous cryptographic system in the Judeo-Christian tradition is the

Atbash substitutions are found in at least two places in the Old Testament. The first two appear in Jeremiah 25:26 and 51:41, where the word 'SHESHACH' is used in place of 'Babel' (Babylon). In Jeremiah 51:1, the phrase LEB KAMAI appears in place of Kashdim.

Scholars don't think that the aim of Atbash transformations was necessarily to hide meaning. Instead, it is thought to be a method of revealing certain interpretations of the Torah.

Other often-discussed 'codes' in the Bible relate to **gematria**, a method of Torah analysis that assigns number values to letters, adds them up and interprets the results. Perhaps the most famous of these is 666, the number referred to as the number of the beast in Revelation 13:18. Some experts believe the number might actually refer to 'Nero Caesar,' transliterated into Hebrew from the Greek (Neron Kaiser).

Another example arises in Genesis 14:14, where the verse describes how Abraham musters 318 of his retainers to go into battle to rescue his cousin, Lot, who had been captured. In Rabbinic tradition, the number 318 is taken as gematria for Eliezer, Abraham's servant. This suggests that Abraham managed the great feat of rescuing his kinsman not with an army of 318 soldiers, but perhaps accompanied only by a solitary servant, albeit one whose name means 'God is my guide'.

One form of Bible analysis that has been widely criticised is that described in Michael Drosnin's book *The Bible Code*. Drosnin wrote that hidden messages could be found in the Bible by looking for equidistant letter sequences.

The book, which drew on the work of mathematician Eliyahu Rips and others, said this procedure unveiled hidden references to various incidents, such as scientific breakthroughs and assassinations.

Above: Biblical depiction of King Nimrod of Babylon and the building of the Tower of Babel. Babel is one of the examples of Atbash substitutions in the Bible.

However, as far as professional cryptanalysts are concerned, the Torah code theory is highly dubious. The lack of vowels in Hebrew, for a start, allows quite a degree of flexibility. Also, because the proportion of letters within a language is fairly strict, any two books of roughly the same length are approximate anagrams – or rearrangements – of each other, and therefore any letter sequences code would not be unique to the Bible. One group of researchers even claimed to have achieved similar results by analysing Herman Melville's *Moby Dick*.

Above: Baphomet, the horned idol of heretical worship.

Baphomet: The Atbash Cipher Theory

For devotees of black magic and the occult, the name Baphomet conjures images of a particularly nasty demon – perhaps even Satan himself – who appears in the guise of a human figure with a goat's horns and wings.

But these associations are relatively recent, not really arising until the 1800s, when a French author and magician called Eliphas Levi popularised an image of Baphomet as a goat-headed figure with wings and breasts.

In fact, the name Baphomet first came to public awareness hundreds of years previously, in the earliest years of the fourteenth century, at a time when members of the Knights Templar were facing accusations of taking part in demonic acts such as worshipping idols.

On Friday 13 October 1307, Philip IV of France had the Templar Grand Master Jacques de Molay and 140 other knights arrested in the Paris Temple. After suffering horrendous torture, members of the order admitted to spitting on, trampling and urinating on the crucifix; an initiation ceremony involving 'obscene kisses'; accepting members through bribery; and worshipping idols, including one known as Baphomet. As a result, many were burned at the stake or fled the country.

Where the name Baphomet came from is shrouded in some mystery, and several possible explanations have been offered. One widely accepted interpretation is that Baphomet was an Old French deformation of 'Mahomet', a version of Muhammad, the name of the prophet of Islam.

Other suggestions are that Baphomet comes from the Greek words 'Baphe' and 'Metis', which together would mean 'Baptism of Wisdom', or that it comprises the abbreviations *Temp. ohp. Ab.*, which originates from the Latin *Templi omnium hominum pacis abhas*, meaning 'the father of universal peace among men'.

But Hugh Schonfield, one of the original researchers working on the Dead Sea Scrolls, raised the most intriguing suggestion.

Schonfield believed that 'Baphomet' was created with knowledge of the Atbash substitution cipher, which replaces the first letter of the Hebrew alphabet for the last, the second for the second-last and so on. If this was the case, then 'Baphomet,' rendered in Hebrew and interpreted using Atbash, becomes something that can be interpreted as the Greek word 'Sophia', or wisdom.

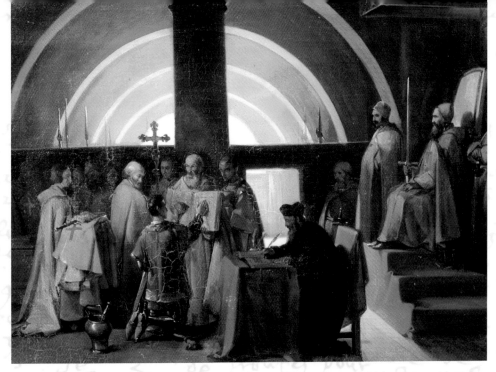

Above: Knight's Templar at worship. Bottom right: Templar Grand Master Jacques de Molay

ב פ ו מ ת

[taf] [mem] [vav] [pe] [bet]

Baphomet in Hebrew right to left.

Applying the Atbash cipher to the name, Schonfield revealed the following:

ש ו פ י א

[alef] [yud] [pe] [vav] [shin]

The Greek word Sophia written in Hebrew right to left.

At this point, the associations begin to get even more esoteric, as some people go even further to make the connection to the Gnostic goddess Sophia, the divine feminine. Sophia, in turn, is sometimes equated with Mary Magdalene, a devoted follower of Jesus Christ.

HOMOPHONES

By the beginning of the fifteenth century, there were signs that cryptanalysts were at work in Europe. In a cipher prepared for the Duchy of Mantua, each plaintext vowel was given a number of different equivalents. This type of cipher, known as a **homophonic substitution**, is more difficult for the codebreaker, requiring more ingenuity and perseverance to crack than simple monoalphabetic ciphers. Its arrival is seen as a clear sign that Mantua's cipher secretary was locked in a battle with someone who might try to solve an intercepted letter, and suggests that he knew something about the principles of frequency analysis.

Homophonic ciphers need more cipher equivalents than there are letters in the alphabet, so various solutions were used to invent larger alphabets. One example is to use numerals in the substitution. In other cases, it might mean using variations on the existing alphabet – uppercase, lowercase or upside down, for example.

Here's an example of a homophonic substitution. The letters along the top row are the plaintext alphabet and the numbers below the alternative cipher options.

a	b	c	d	e	f	g	h	i	j	k	l	m	n	o	p	q	r	s	t	u	v	w	x	y	z
46	04	55	14	09	48	74	36	13	10	16	24	15	07	22	76	30	08	12	01	17	06	66	57	67	26
52	20		97	31	73	85	37	18	38		29	60	23	63	95		34	27	19	32				71	
58			39				61	47			49		54	41			42	64	35						
79			50				68	70									53		78						
91			65																93						
			69																						
			96																						

Using this cipher, the plaintext 'This is the beginning' could be written as:

01361312 1827 193731 043974470723705485

Cracking a homophonic cipher

Although homophones can successfully hide the frequencies of individual letters, those of two- or three-letter combinations are not concealed so well, particularly in long stretches of ciphertext.

One basic method for cracking homophonic ciphers is to examine the cryptogram for partial repetitions. For example, if in a ciphertext the two sequences:

2052644755

and

2058644755

both occurred, a cryptanalyst might wonder whether '52' and '58' were homophones for the same plaintext letter.

Also, a cryptanalyst who knew that the most common two- and three-letter combinations within words are 'th', 'in', 'he', 'er' and 'the', 'ing' and 'and', might find that the symbol 37 is often preceded by 19 and followed by 39.

Taking a guess, this might suggest that 19 represents 't', 37 'h' and 39 'e.' By continuing this process, the secrets of the message can painstakingly be revealed.

THE DEATH OF MARY, QUEEN OF SCOTS

In 1587, England's most accomplished cryptanalyst used frequency analysis to send a sovereign to her death and decide the future of a nation. Mary, Queen of Scots had ruled Scotland until 1567, when she abdicated and fled to England. But her cousin, Queen Elizabeth I, saw the Catholic Mary, grand-niece of Henry VIII, as a grave threat and had her imprisoned in a series of castles around the country. Anti-Catholic laws set down by Elizabeth had created a climate of fear in the country, and the imprisoned Mary became a focus for civil unrest and plots to depose the Protestant Queen.

In 1586, a devotee of Mary's, Anthony Babington, began plotting to assassinate Elizabeth and install Mary on the throne. The success of the plot relied on Mary's cooperation, but communicating with her secretly was no easy task.

So, Babington recruited a former seminarian, Gilbert Gifford, as messenger and the young, daring Gifford soon found a way of using a beer barrel to smuggle letters in and out of Mary's prison at the country estate of Chartley.

But Gifford was a double agent. He had pledged his allegiance to Elizabeth's principal secretary, Sir Francis Walsingham – the founder of England's first secret service. The former seminarian was delivering Mary's letters straight to England's master codebreaker, Thomas Phelippes.

Much of Mary's communication with the outside world was encrypted, but that was only a minor problem for Phelippes, a slender, short-sighted man whose face bore the tell-tale marks of smallpox infection. He was reputed to be fluent in French, Spanish, Italian and Latin, and was also a notoriously skillful forger.

Walsingham's top cryptanalyst was a master of frequency analysis, and this skill allowed him to reveal the secrets of messages passed between the imprisoned Mary and Babington.

On the basis of the evidence that Phelippes helped gather, Walsingham tried to persuade Elizabeth that the throne and her life were in danger unless she had Mary executed. The English queen refused, but Walsingham was convinced that if evidence existed that Mary was plotting assassination, Elizabeth would agree to order her execution.

On 6 July, Babington wrote a long letter to Mary revealing the details of what has become known as the Babington Plot. He asked for Mary's approval and advice to ensure 'the dispatch of the usurping Competitor' – the assassination of Elizabeth I.

When Mary replied on 17 July, she sealed her fate. Walsingham asked the skilled Phelippes to copy the letter and add a forged postscript in code asking for the identities of the plotters.

The names were duly supplied, and their fate, too, was sealed. Mary's involvement in the plot had been proven. Walsingham could now move

Above: Queen Elizabeth 1, (1533 to 1603), Queen of England, Queen of France (in name only) and Queen of Ireland from 17 November 1558 until her death.

Left: Mary 1 of Scotland (1542 to 1587), better known as Mary, Queen of Scots. Her death at the hands of Elizabeth 1 has become a mainstay of cryptographic history.

decisively. Within days, Babington and his colleagues were arrested and taken to the Tower of London. Mary was put on trial in October. Elizabeth signed her death warrant on 1 February 1587, and seven days later she was beheaded in the Great Hall at Fotheringay.

The messages that Gilbert Gifford was smuggling out of Chartley in casks of ale – and delivering straight into the hands of Thomas

Right: Thomas Phelippes' forged cipher postscript to Mary, Queen of Scots' letter to Anthony Babington, asking him to reveal the names of the conspirators.

Phelippes – had been encrypted by Mary's cipher secretary Gilbert Curle, who used a range of different nomenclators and 'nulls' – these represented nothing and were introduced as red herrings to confuse the codebreaker – for his encryption.

Nonetheless, Mary's codes stood no chance in the face of Phelippe's mastery of frequency analysis. With a combination of perseverance, careful guesswork and pure luck it is possible to fill in the blanks and crack the code. For skilled cryptanalysts this is second nature – in the case of Thomas Phelippes, it is recorded that he was able to decode Mary's letters almost as soon as he received them.

PUTTING FREQUENCY ANALYSIS INTO PRACTICE

For a cryptanalyst confronted with a piece of enciphered text, one of the first challenges is to figure out what sort of transformation has been performed on the original message. Without any other clues, frequency analysis can help clarify what you are dealing with.

In a transposition cipher, for example, the frequencies of the letters will be exactly the same as in the plaintext – they haven't been replaced, simply jumbled up, so 'e' will still be the most common letter and so on. Substitutions, on the other hand, will have different frequencies – that is, whatever replaced 'e' might become the most frequent letter.

Let's suppose you're trying to crack the following piece of ciphertext, and all you knew was that the original plaintext message was in English:

YCKKVOTM OTZU OZGRE IGKYGX QTKC ZNGZ NK CGY XOYQOTM
CUXRJ CGX LUX NK NGJ IUTLKYYKJ GY SAIN ZU NOY
IUSVGTOUTY GTJ YNAJJKXKJ GZ ZNK VXUYVKIZ IRKGX YOMNZKJ
GY NK CGY NUCKBKX TUZ KBKT IGKYGX IUARJ GTZOIOVGZK ZNK
LARR IUTYKWAKTIKY UL NOY JKIOYOUT

First, complete a frequency count for the letters in the ciphertext. A good way to do this is to write the alphabet out along the bottom of a piece of paper, and when you encounter that letter put an 'X' above it, building a kind of graph.

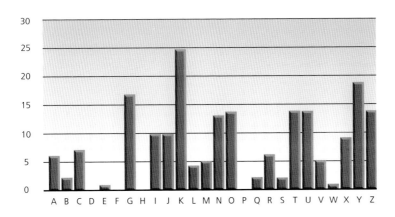

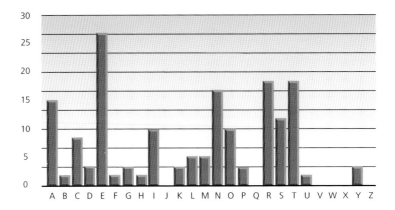

Now compare the completed chart to a graph we derived earlier from the standard distribution of letters in English.

Immediately, it is clear that in the ciphertext, there are hardly any 'e's – suggesting it isn't a simple transposition. However, the letter frequency in the ciphertext does have some similarities to the standard frequencies. Look at the letter K, for example. It is by far the most common letter – which could suggest it has replaced 'e' in the cipher.

There are other clues – for example, in the patterns that follow the K. There are two peaks at N and O, followed by another at T–U. Then there are three relatively high peaks at X, Y and Z.

Experienced cryptanalysts might recognise that 2–2–3 peak pattern. In plain English, those peaks occur at the letters H and I, N and O and R, S and T.

In fact, the whole graph looks a little like it has been shifted along six places to the right. Which indeed it has. The text was enciphered using a Caesar shift of six places.

So, by taking each letter of the ciphertext and moving it back six places in the alphabet, Y becomes S, C becomes W and so on, until:

YCKKVOTM OTZU OZGRE IGKYGX QTKC ZNGZ NK CGY XOYQOTM CUXRJ CGX LUX NK NGJ IUTLKYYKJ GY SAIN ZU NOY IUSVGTOUTY GTJ YNAJJKXKJ GZ ZNK VXUYVKIZ IRKGX YOMNZKJ GY NK CGY NUCKBKX TUZ KBKT IGKYGX IUARJ GTZOIOVGZK ZNK LARR IUTYKWAKTIKY UL NOY JKIOYOUT

is revealed to be an excerpt from Tom Holland's book, *Rubicon*:

> *Sweeping into Italy, Caesar knew that he was risking world war for he had confessed as much to his companions and shuddered at the prospect. Clear-sighted as he was however, not even Caesar could anticipate the full consequences of his decision.*

CODES OF THE KAMA SUTRA

In modern parlance, the *Kama Sutra* is a kind of synonym for sex manual, as emphasised by the profusion of illustrated versions, videos and websites devoted to its suggestions.

But the *Kama Sutra of Vatsyayana* (Aphorisms on Love), to use its full name, is much more than simply a guide to exotic positions for lovemaking. As well as defining the three types of men and women according to the dimensions of their privates (hare, bull or horse for men; doe, mare or elephant for women) it is also a complete beginner's guide to love, romance, marriage and more.

The *Kama Sutra* also places some importance on women developing the skills of cryptography and cryptanalysis. Number 41 on the list of essential arts is the ability to solve riddles, enigmas and use covert speech. Following it is *Mlecchita vikalpa*, 'the art of understanding writing in cipher and the writing of words in a peculiar way'.

The book has a couple of practical illustrations of techniques that might be used, including the verbal tricks of changing the beginning and end of words or adding letters between syllables. In writing, it mentions 'arranging the words of a verse written irregularly by separating vowels from consonants or leaving them out altogether'.

An important commentary on the *Kama Sutra*, Yasodhara's *Jayamangala*, written around 1000 CE, includes various forms of a system that might be used. In his tome *The Code Breakers*, David Kahn describes one of these as *kautiliyam*, in which letters are substituted according to phonetic relationships, with vowels, for example, becoming consonants.

Another of the methods listed is *Muladeviya*. In this system, several of the letters of the alphabet are exchanged, while the rest remain the same.

a	kh	gh.	c	t	ñ	n	r	l	y
k	g	n	t.	p	n.	m	s.	s	-

'If a wife becomes separated from her husband, and falls into distress, she can support herself easily, even in a foreign country, by means of her knowledge of these arts,' Vatsyayana suggests. 'A man who is versed in these arts, is loquacious and acquainted with the arts of gallantry.'

While some of the suggestions of the *Kama Sutra* might seem odd in the modern world, the advice about secret writing isn't ever likely to go out of fashion. As lovers throughout the ages can attest – from Romeo and Juliet to Prince Charles and Camilla – there's nothing more embarrassing than having your romantic words revealed to the world outside the bedroom.

CHAPTER TWO

INGENUITY

How mad monks, diplomats and papal advisors
turned cryptology on its head.
Plus, the arrival of the codebreaking civil servants.

The use of frequency analysis shattered the security that simple ciphers had once offered. This meant that anyone using monoalphabetic substitution systems faced the prospect of their messages being deciphered and read by their enemies.

The codebreakers might have gained an advantage, but not for long. A series of brilliant European amateurs had already set the next development in motion, creating a form of cipher that was vastly more resistant to the techniques that counted letter frequency.

PAPAL ENCRYPTION

This new form of cipher can be traced to the papal court and was the product of the extraordinary mind of Leon Battista Alberti, the illegitimate son of a wealthy Florentine. Alberti was a genuine Renaissance man whose talents encompassed architecture, the arts, science and the law. He was also, by all accounts, a codebreaker extraordinaire. One day, Alberti was strolling in the gardens of the Vatican with his friend Leonardo Dato, pontifical secretary, when the

Opposite: Leon Battista Alberti, Renaissance man and codebreaker extraordinaire who invented the cipher disc.

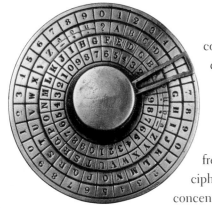

Above: A nineteenth-century cipher disc based on Alberti's original concept of cipher discs.

conversation turned to the subject of ciphers. Dato confessed that the Vatican needed to send encrypted messages – and Alberti promised to help. As a result, it seems, he wrote an essay in or around 1467 that laid the foundations for a completely new way of writing in cipher.

Alberti's essay included a clear explanation of frequency analysis and offered various means for solving ciphers. It also described a system of encryption using two concentric metal discs whose circumferences were divided into 24 equal parts. The segments of the outer disc contained the letters of the alphabet and numbers 1 to 4 (he left out h, k and y – and j, u and w were not in the Latin alphabet). The cells of the inner circle contained the 24 letters of the Latin alphabet (lacking U, W and J, with 'et' added) in random order.

To send an encrypted letter, the letters or numbers in a plaintext message were read on the outer plate and were replaced with the corresponding letter on the inner plate. The sender and the receiver both needed to have identical discs and decide on an initial position for the two discs relative to each other.

Up to this point, the system is just a monoalphabetic substitution. But in what he wrote next, Alberti took an ingenious step forward. 'After writing three or four words,' he said, 'I shall change the position of the index in our formula by turning the circle.'

This may not sound like much, but its consequences were important. For the first few letters, the ciphertext 'k' on the inner circle might, for instance, correspond to the plaintext 'f', but once the discs were spun, ciphertext 'k' might suddenly then stand for 't', or any other letter for that matter.

These circumstances made things a great deal harder for codebreakers. Each new position of the discs brought new correlations between ciphertexts and plaintexts, meaning (to take an English example) the word 'cat' might have been 'gdi' in one instance, and 'alx' in another. The usefulness of frequency analysis was therefore greatly diminished.

In addition, Alberti used the numbers on the outer ring as a kind of enciphered code. That is, before enciphering the plaintext, he would substitute certain phrases with combinations of the numbers from 1 to 4 according to a small code-book. Those numbers would then be enciphered along with the rest of the message.

CODE ANALYSIS

Let's imagine Alberti wanted to send the message: Tell Pope at once eleven ships will sail in the morning.

First, he would have replaced certain words and phrases in the message according to an agreed code-book. For this exercise, let's say that 14 stands for 'ships will sail in the morning' and 342 replaces 'Pope'.

To encipher the message, first replace the phrases with their code-groups. This gives: Tell 342 at once eleven 14. Then, using the cipher-disc in the first position, encipher the first three words:

Plaintext	tell	342	at	Once	eleven	14
Ciphertext	IZOO	MRET	DI			

Now, the disc changes position, changing the association between the plain alphabet and the cipher alphabet. For the purpose of this exercise, let's shift the outer disc one cell anti-clockwise. Then carry on and encipher the rest of the message.

Plaintext	Tell	342	at	Once	eleven	14
Ciphertext	IZOO	MRET	DI	FSGA	ABAIAS	ETD

This gives the final ciphertext as: IZOO MRET DI FSGA ABAIAS ETD

You will see from looking at this example that the plaintext **e** in the word 'tell' is replaced by **Z** – but once we reach the e in the word 'once' it has been replaced by **A**. The same thing happens to I, which is **O** in the early words, but **B** later on. Also, early in the message the ciphertext **ET** replaces **2**, while later it stands for **1**. For a cryptanalyst, this kind of change presented a real challenge.

ROSSLYN'S SECRETS: HIDDEN MEANING IN ARCHITECTURE AND MUSIC

Throughout history, artists have enriched their works with hidden meaning, codes and symbols. Mozart is thought to have included Masonic references in some of his operas, for example, while the paintings of Leonardo da Vinci often seem rich with subtle subtexts and symbolism.

Architects have also endowed their creations with subtle messages. Perhaps the most enigmatic of these can be found in the small village of Roslin, south of the Scottish capital of Edinburgh. There you will find the extraordinary construction called the Rosslyn chapel.

The architecture of the chapel, whose foundation stone was laid on St. Matthew's Day, 1446, is rich with code and hidden meanings that have mesmerised visitors for centuries. Chief among its attractions is the Apprentice Pillar, which is carved with a distinct and beautiful helical pattern.

Some believe the pillar and its partner, the so-called Master Pillar, signify the pillars of Boaz and Jachin, which stood at the entrance to the first Temple of Jerusalem. On the architrave joining the pillar is a Latin inscription (*Forte est vinum fortior est rex fortiores sunt mulieres super omnia vincit veritas*) whose translation is 'Wine is strong, a King is stronger, women are stronger still, but truth conquers all'. This quotation comes from *Esdras*, chapter 3, from the Biblical Apocrypha.

The chapel also has a long connection with Freemasonry and, according to legend, the Knights Templar. Throughout the church are references to the Key of Hiram, a significant piece of Masonic legend, and in modern times the building has been used for ceremonies by the Masonic group, the modern Knights Templar.

Also, because of its connections with Freemasonry, and rumours of secret vaults below its floor, the chapel has been suggested as a possible final resting place for the Holy Grail. Legend suggests there are three medieval chests buried somewhere on the property, but scanning and excavations in or near the Chapel have not yielded anything.

Opposite: The famous Apprentice's Pillar and, above, the carved interior roof of Rosslyn Chapel.

One exploration, however, has yielded results. In 2005, Scottish composer Stuart Mitchell succeeded in cracking a complex series of codes hidden in 213 cubes on the ceiling of the chapel. After pondering the problem for 20 years, Mitchell found that patterns on the cubes form a piece of music written for 13 medieval players. The unusual sound is thought to have been of spiritual significance to those who built the chapel.

The key to the deciphering came when he discovered that the stones at the bottom of each of 12 pillars inside the chapel formed a cadence – three chords at the end of a piece of music – of which there were only three types known or used in the fifteenth century.

In October 2005, he told *The Scotsman* newspaper: 'It is in triple time, sounds childlike, and is based on plain chant, which was the common form of rhythm of the time. In the 1400s, there wasn't a great deal of guidance for tempo, so I have chosen to make it run for six and a half minutes, but it could be stretched to eight minutes if a different tempo was used.'

The chapel itself gives instructions about the musicians who should play the piece. At the end of each pillar is a musician playing a different medieval instrument – including bagpipes, whistles, trumpet, a medieval mouth piano, guitar and singers. The Edinburgh musician has named the piece The Rosslyn Canon of Proportions.

Alberti's remarkable feats earned him the title of 'the father of western cryptology'. But the evolution of cryptography hadn't stopped there, and the next step in the development of polyalphabetic systems came from the pen of an equally remarkable mind.

TRIMETHIUS' TABLEAU

Johannes Trimethius was a German-born abbott who produced the world's first printed book on cryptography. He was a controversial figure, to say the least, with an interest in occultism that triggered consternation in his friends and outrage in others.

His mammoth contribution to the craft of cryptography took the form of a work on codes and ciphers, entitled *Polygraphia*, which was published as a series of six books after his death in 1516. The work set out what has now become a standard method for writing poly-alphabetic cipher systems, the **tableau**.

CODE ANALYSIS

Opposite is the kind of tableau Trimethius described, using the full English alphabet. His idea was to set out a table that had 26 columns across and 26 rows down. Each row contains an alphabet in standard order, but in each successive row the alphabet undergoes a Caesar shift by one further place (see opposite).

To write an enciphered message, Trimethius suggested using the first row for enciphering the first letter, the second row for the second letter and so on. In terms of making a message impervious to frequency analysis, Trimethius' technique offered significant benefits over Alberti's. In particular, it obscured the repetition of letters within a word, which can be an important clue for codebreakers.

Let's say you want to encipher the message 'All is well' using Trimethius' technique. Use the top row of the table as your plaintext, and, with each letter, use successively lower rows to provide the ciphertext. To illustrate how this works, we can use the table opposite. For the first letter

Trimethius' Tableau

a	b	c	d	e	f	g	h	i	j	k	l	m	n	o	p	q	r	s	t	u	v	w	x	y	z
b	c	d	e	f	g	h	i	j	k	l	m	n	o	p	q	r	s	t	u	v	w	x	y	z	a
c	d	e	f	g	h	i	j	k	l	m	n	o	p	q	r	s	t	u	v	w	x	y	z	a	b
d	e	f	g	h	i	j	k	l	m	n	o	p	q	r	s	t	u	v	w	x	y	z	a	b	c
e	f	g	h	i	j	k	l	m	n	o	p	q	r	s	t	u	v	w	x	y	z	a	b	c	d
f	g	h	i	j	k	l	m	n	o	p	q	r	s	t	u	v	w	x	y	z	a	b	c	d	e
g	h	i	j	k	l	m	n	o	p	q	r	s	t	u	v	w	x	y	z	a	b	c	d	e	f
h	i	j	k	l	m	n	o	p	q	r	s	t	u	v	w	x	y	z	a	b	c	d	e	f	g
i	j	k	l	m	n	o	p	q	r	s	t	u	v	w	x	y	z	a	b	c	d	e	f	g	h
j	k	l	m	n	o	p	q	r	s	t	u	v	w	x	y	z	a	b	c	d	e	f	g	h	i
k	l	m	n	o	p	q	r	s	t	u	v	w	x	y	z	a	b	c	d	e	f	g	h	i	j
l	m	n	o	p	q	r	s	t	u	v	w	x	y	z	a	b	c	d	e	f	g	h	i	j	k
m	n	o	p	q	r	s	t	u	v	w	x	y	z	a	b	c	d	e	f	g	h	i	j	k	l
n	o	p	q	r	s	t	u	v	w	x	y	z	a	b	c	d	e	f	g	h	i	j	k	l	m
o	p	q	r	s	t	u	v	w	x	y	z	a	b	c	d	e	f	g	h	i	j	k	l	m	n
p	q	r	s	t	u	v	w	x	y	z	a	b	c	d	e	f	g	h	i	j	k	l	m	n	o
q	r	s	t	u	v	w	x	y	z	a	b	c	d	e	f	g	h	i	j	k	l	m	n	o	p
r	s	t	u	v	w	x	y	z	a	b	c	d	e	f	g	h	i	j	k	l	m	n	o	p	q
s	t	u	v	w	x	y	z	a	b	c	d	e	f	g	h	i	j	k	l	m	n	o	p	q	r
t	u	v	w	x	y	z	a	b	c	d	e	f	g	h	i	j	k	l	m	n	o	p	q	r	s
u	v	w	x	y	z	a	b	c	d	e	f	g	h	i	j	k	l	m	n	o	p	q	r	s	t
v	w	x	y	z	a	b	c	d	e	f	g	h	i	j	k	l	m	n	o	p	q	r	s	t	u
w	x	y	z	a	b	c	d	e	f	g	h	i	j	k	l	m	n	o	p	q	r	s	t	u	v
x	y	z	a	b	c	d	e	f	g	h	i	j	k	l	m	n	o	p	q	r	s	t	u	v	w
y	z	a	b	c	d	e	f	g	h	i	j	k	l	m	n	o	p	q	r	s	t	u	v	w	x
z	a	b	c	d	e	f	g	h	i	j	k	l	m	n	o	p	q	r	s	t	u	v	w	x	y

Enciphered message 'All is well'

A	b	c	d	e	f	g	h	i	j	k	l	m	n	o	p	q	r	s	t	u	v	w	x	y	z
b	c	d	e	f	g	h	i	j	k	l	**M**	n	o	p	q	r	s	t	u	v	w	x	y	z	a
c	d	e	f	g	h	i	j	k	l	m	**N**	o	p	q	r	s	t	u	v	w	x	y	z	a	b
d	e	f	g	h	i	j	k	**L**	m	n	o	p	q	r	s	t	u	v	w	x	y	z	a	b	c
e	f	g	h	i	j	k	l	m	n	o	p	q	r	s	t	u	v	**W**	x	y	z	a	b	c	d
f	g	h	i	j	k	l	m	n	o	p	q	r	s	t	u	v	w	x	y	z	a	**B**	c	d	e
g	h	i	j	**K**	l	m	n	o	p	q	r	s	t	u	v	w	x	y	z	a	b	c	d	e	f
h	i	j	k	l	m	n	o	p	q	r	**S**	t	u	v	w	x	y	z	a	b	c	d	e	f	g
i	j	k	l	m	n	o	p	q	r	s	**T**	u	v	w	x	y	z	a	b	c	d	e	f	g	h

in the plaintext, we take the letter **a** from the first row. For the second, follow the column headed by **I** down to the second row. For the following **I**, trace down to the third row. The process continues until the message is enciphered (see previous page).

So the encrypted message is: **AMN LW BKST**. Notice that neither of the repeated Is appear as repetitions in the ciphertext.

Over the next few decades of the sixteenth century, the ideas behind polyalphabetic ciphers went through further refinements, but the man whose name has permanently been stuck to the tableau form of cipher was Blaise de Vigenère – a Frenchman born in 1523.

THE VIGENÈRE CIPHER

Vigenère, a French diplomat, first came into contact with cryptography in 1549 at the age of 26 while on a two-year mission in Rome. In those years, he read the works of Alberti, Trimethius and other

Left: Rome, the city that first introduced Vigenère to cryptography.

THE MOST MYSTERIOUS BOOK:
THE VOYNICH MANUSCRIPT

Above: A page from the Voynich manuscript.

In the year 1639, an alchemist from Prague by the name of Georg Baresch wrote a letter to the renowned Jesuit scholar Athanasius Kircher, pleading for his help in deciphering a book that had been puzzling him for years. The manuscript, illustrated on almost every page with intricate, but obscure, drawings, appeared to have something to do with alchemy, but was written in a mysterious, incomprehensible script.

Knowing that Kircher had 'deciphered' the Egyptian hieroglyphs, Baresch hoped that he would be able to unlock the secrets of his mystifying book and sent copies of it to him in Rome. But Kircher, it seems, was as perplexed by the book as Baresch, and no solution was forthcoming.

In fact, during the more than 360 years that have passed since then, it has become plain that the failure of these two seventeenth-century scholars was nothing to be embarrassed about. Because the Voynich manuscript – named after the Polish booklover Wilfrid Voynich, who rediscovered it in the library of a Jesuit college near Rome in 1912 – remains an utter mystery.

The book, six inches wide and nine high, contains 232 pages, almost all of which are intricately illustrated with stars, plants and human figures. On some pages, the text swirls around in a spiral, while on others it is arranged in blocks around the edges of the page. In many cases the words seem to have been squeezed into the space left after a complex drawing was laid on the page.

Since being unearthed in the second decade of last century, the Voynich manuscript has attracted the attention of some of the best cryptanalytical minds around. Toward the end of World War II, for example, William F. Friedman (known as the man who broke the Japanese diplomatic cipher, Purple) tried to crack it in an after-hours club of US Army cryptanalysts. They failed, as have so many others.

That's not to say, of course, that more or less spurious 'solutions' haven't been advertised. Some have suggested that the book contains

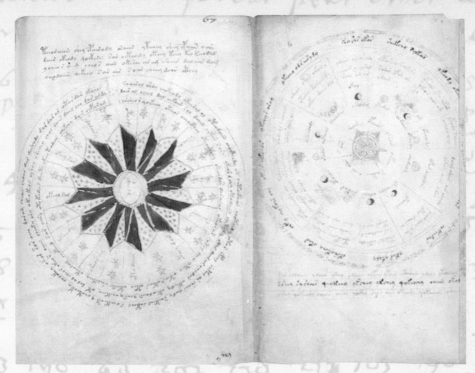

Opposite and above: Nature and alchemy, the enciphered Voynich manuscript.

discoveries and inventions by the thirteenth-century friar, Roger Bacon. Others suggest it is a prayer book from the Cathars, which escaped destruction during the Inquisition and was written in a pidgin version of a Germanic/Romance creole.

Others have suggested the book is a hoax – perhaps it is gibberish written by a medieval Italian charlatan to impress his clientele – although the length and complexity of the text, together with the convincing patterns of repetition in the letters used, argue against this.

More than three centuries on, the book retains its appeal. René Zandbergen, a scientist from the European Space Agency, has been fascinated by the book for the last 15 years. Part of its intrigue, he says, is that it looks like it ought to be simple to crack, but has eluded so many fine minds.

Zandbergen doesn't consider himself a cryptanalyst, but his historical detective-work has unveiled several of the manuscript's secrets, including correspondence that throws light on its history. In his view, the book is most likely meaningless, a piece of nonsense dating back some 500 years or more.

'If it isn't a hoax, the only thing I can think is that the words in the book are more like a numbering system,' he says, which would make it more of a code than a cipher. In which case, decryption would rely on finding its code-book or some other documentation hidden in one of Europe's ancient libraries.

Either way, there's little sign that interest is waning in the Voynich Manuscript, which currently resides in Yale University's Beinecke Rare Book and Manuscript Library. It is still the subject of intense scrutiny from codebreakers around the world. Perhaps all their work will one day result in the code being cracked. Then again, perhaps not.

important figures, and perhaps came to know some of the Vatican's codebreaking insiders.

Some 20 years later, Vigenère retired from court life and began writing. Among his more than 20 books is the famed *Traicté des Chiffres*, which was first published in 1586.

CODE ANALYSIS

Vigenère's book took another important step forward in the development of polyalphabetic ciphers by suggesting a variety of **keys** that could be used to decide which rows of a tableau to use when enciphering a message. Instead of simply cycling through the different cipher alphabets, the person sending a message would use them in a specific order – for example, if the word 'cipher' was used as the key, then the tableau rows beginning with **c, i, p, h, e** and **r** would be used in sequence to encipher the message.

To encrypt a message in this way, write the plaintext out with the keyword repeated above it. Each letter of the message is enciphered using the tableau row that begins with the corresponding letter of the key.

Key	c i p h e r c i p h e r c i
Plaintext	a v o i d n o r t h p a s s
Ciphertext	C D D P H E Q C I O T S Q A

Say your plaintext is 'avoid north pass'. To encipher the first letter, **a**, you use the row that starts with **c**, the letter of the key you have written above it.

To do this, look on the tableau opposite at the column topped by the letter **a**, and run your finger down to where it intersects with the row beginning with **c**. This gives your ciphertext as **C**. For the second letter of the message, the process is exactly the same – run your finger down the column starting with **v** until you reach the row beginning with the letter **i** and you have your ciphertext, which is **D**.

Above: Blaise de Vigenère (1523 to 1596), French diplomat and cryptographer.

Polyalphabetic ciphers

a	b	c	d	e	f	g	h	i	j	k	l	m	n	o	p	q	r	s	t	u	v	w	x	y	z
b	c	d	e	f	g	h	i	j	k	l	m	n	o	p	q	r	s	t	u	v	w	x	y	z	a
C	d	e	f	g	h	i	j	k	l	m	n	o	p	q	r	s	t	u	v	w	x	y	z	a	b
d	e	f	g	h	i	j	k	l	m	n	o	p	q	r	s	t	u	v	w	x	y	z	a	b	c
e	f	g	h	i	j	k	l	m	n	o	p	q	r	s	t	u	v	w	x	y	z	a	b	c	d
f	g	h	i	j	k	l	m	n	o	p	q	r	s	t	u	v	w	x	y	z	a	b	c	d	e
g	h	i	j	k	l	m	n	o	p	q	r	s	t	u	v	w	x	y	z	a	b	c	d	e	f
h	i	j	k	l	m	n	o	p	q	r	s	t	u	v	w	x	y	z	a	b	c	d	e	f	g
i	j	k	l	m	n	o	p	q	r	s	t	u	v	w	x	y	z	a	b	c	**D**	e	f	g	h
j	k	l	m	n	o	p	q	r	s	t	u	v	w	x	y	z	a	b	c	d	e	f	g	h	i
k	l	m	n	o	p	q	r	s	t	u	v	w	x	y	z	a	b	c	d	e	f	g	h	i	j
l	m	n	o	p	q	r	s	t	u	v	w	x	y	z	a	b	c	d	e	f	g	h	i	j	k
m	n	o	p	q	r	s	t	u	v	w	x	y	z	a	b	c	d	e	f	g	h	i	j	k	l
n	o	p	q	r	s	t	u	v	w	x	y	z	a	b	c	d	e	f	g	h	i	j	k	l	m
o	p	q	r	s	t	u	v	w	x	y	z	a	b	c	d	e	f	g	h	i	j	k	l	m	n
p	q	r	s	t	u	v	w	x	y	z	a	b	c	d	e	f	g	h	i	j	k	l	m	n	o
q	r	s	t	u	v	w	x	y	z	a	b	c	d	e	f	g	h	i	j	k	l	m	n	o	p
r	s	t	u	v	w	x	y	z	a	b	c	d	e	f	g	h	i	j	k	l	m	n	o	p	q
s	t	u	v	w	x	y	z	a	b	c	d	e	f	g	h	l	j	k	l	m	n	o	p	q	r
t	u	v	w	x	y	z	a	b	c	d	e	f	g	h	i	j	k	l	m	n	o	p	q	r	s
u	v	w	x	y	z	a	b	c	d	e	f	g	h	i	j	k	l	m	n	o	p	q	r	s	t
v	w	x	y	z	a	b	c	d	e	f	g	h	i	j	k	l	m	n	o	p	q	r	s	t	u
w	x	y	z	a	b	c	d	e	f	g	h	i	j	k	l	m	n	o	p	q	r	s	t	u	v
x	y	z	a	b	c	d	e	f	g	h	i	j	k	l	m	n	o	p	q	r	s	t	u	v	w
y	z	a	b	c	d	e	f	g	h	i	j	k	l	m	n	o	p	q	r	s	t	u	v	w	x
z	a	b	c	d	e	f	g	h	i	j	k	l	m	n	o	p	q	r	s	t	u	v	w	x	y

Polyalphabetic ciphers

a	b	c	d	e	f	g	h	i	j	k	l	m	n	o	p	q	r	s	t	u	v	w	x	y	z
b	c	d	e	f	g	h	i	j	k	l	m	n	o	p	q	r	s	t	u	v	w	x	y	z	a
C	d	e	f	g	h	i	j	k	l	m	n	o	p	q	r	s	t	u	v	w	x	y	z	a	b
d	e	f	g	h	i	j	k	l	m	n	o	p	q	r	s	t	u	v	w	x	y	z	a	b	c
e	f	g	h	i	j	k	l	m	n	o	p	q	r	s	t	u	v	w	x	y	z	a	b	c	d
f	g	h	i	j	k	l	m	n	o	p	q	r	s	t	u	v	w	x	y	z	a	b	c	d	e
g	h	i	j	k	l	m	n	o	p	q	r	s	t	u	v	w	x	y	z	a	b	c	d	e	f
h	i	j	k	l	m	n	o	p	q	r	s	t	u	v	w	x	y	z	a	b	c	d	e	f	g
i	j	k	l	m	n	o	p	q	r	s	t	u	v	w	x	y	z	a	b	c	**D**	e	f	g	h

CRACKING POLYALPHABETIC CIPHERS

Although polyalphabetic ciphers can't be cracked simply by using frequency analysis, you can still gain some valuable clues about the nature of the cipher you're dealing with by counting the frequency of letters in a piece of enciphered text.

For a start, polyalphabetic ciphers tend to give a much flatter distribution of letters without the distinctive peaks and troughs of normal distribution.

Take this piece of plaintext for example:

Aerial reconnaissance reports enemy reinforcements estimated at battalion strength entering your sector PD Clarke.

If you count the number of times each letter of the alphabet appears, and plot it on a graph, the result looks like this:

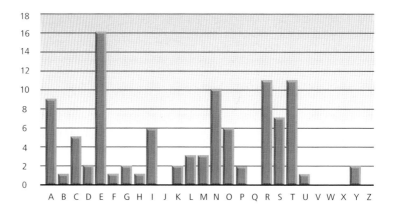

A simple substitution might give the following ciphertext:

LWVOL QVWAT DOLOH HLDAW VWPTV FHWDW RSVWO DNTVA
WRWDF HWHFO RLFWK LFJLF FLQOT DHFVW DMFBW DFWVO
DMSTX VHWAF TVPKA QLVCW

If you count the frequency of each letter for this text, and plot it on another graph, it looks like this (note there are still many letters that stand out as being much more common than others):

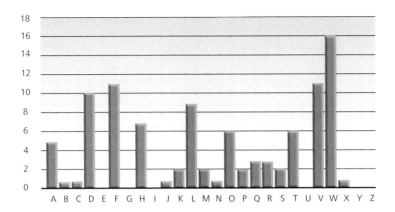

However, a polyalphabetic substitution might give the following ciphertext:

TARAB CZPNW TNNLL ZEFNM KLNHF OWWQM PEPVM NKRXK
QNPRB FXZXE MBXEO LFJML RWPZS GZXSS EUZYS IXWRV QZFSG
FEITT HYHRW EGIKF

Suddenly the graph starts looking much flatter:

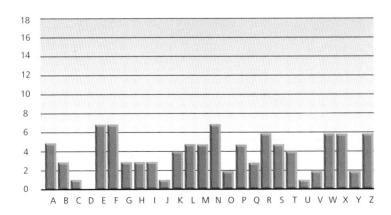

This flatness is a clue that the cipher system involved may be a polyalphabetic one. Once you have this clue, the next hurdle is trying to figure out the cipher's key.

This might be a repeating key, for example the word 'titus', or it could be continuous, such as a long piece of poetry, perhaps *Xanadu* by Samuel Taylor Coleridge.

The trick to spotting a repeating key is to look for repeated sequences of letters in the ciphertext. Say, for example, the plaintext message 'report at zero two zero tomorrow' is enciphered with a Vigenère square using the key 'titus'.

Key	titus	titus	titus	Titus	Titus	titus
Plain	repor	tatze	rotwo	Twoze	Rotom	orrow
Cipher	KMIIJ	MIMTW	KWMQG	MEHTW	KWMIE	HZKIO

The ciphertext would be:

KMIIJMIM<u>TWKW</u>MQGMEH<u>TWKW</u>MIEHZKIO

The cryptanalyst might notice that the letters TWKW turn up twice in the ciphertext, giving a clue that perhaps this is because the same stretch of plaintext has been enciphered using the same letters in the key.

Counting from the start of the first occurrence to the start of the next is a distance of 10 characters. For a codebreaker this information could be priceless, as it shows that the key must be either 10 characters long, or a length that divides into 10, such as 2 or 5 characters long.

As it turns out, the repetition has occurred because then the word 'zero' happened to fall at the same place in the key word 'titus', thus generating the same ciphertext both times.

Of course, such clues aren't always available, and the canny cryptanalyst needs a multitude of other tools at his or her disposal. These might include taking guesses at the length of the key and searching for letter frequencies by position in the suspected key length, and other techniques. Suffice to say, the process is laborious, and requires plenty of imagination and a capacity for seemingly endless perseverance.

THE AGE OF THE BLACK CHAMBERS

The Vigenère cipher is significantly more difficult to crack than monoalphabetic ciphers. And yet historians of cryptography know that polyalphabetic ciphers didn't become widely used for hundreds of years. Nomenclators kept their place as the method of choice in the vast majority of cases, probably because polyalphabetic ciphers, although highly secure, were slow to use and prone to inaccuracies.

In fact, one of the most skilled cryptographers of history crafted a long and successful career from his ability to construct tricky nomenclators. His name was Antoine Rossignol, born in 1600, who became France's first full-time cryptologist and subject of the first poem written to a cryptologist – composed by his friend, the poet Boisrobert.

Rossignol was a central figure in the court of King Louis XIII and was famed primarily for his role as the most skilled cryptanalyst in Europe, although he was also a talented cryptographer.

He first came to the attention of the king and his court in 1626 when he quickly deciphered a letter snatched from a messenger leaving the besieged city of Réalmont. His decipherment showed that the Huguenot forces in control of the city were in desperate need of supplies and on the brink of capitulating – it was returned, decoded, to the citizens of the city, and they surrendered, allowing the royal army an unexpectedly simple victory.

Above: Louis XIII (1601 to 1643), called *le Juste* (the Just), was King of France from 1610 to 1643.

This was the sort of gift that Louis and his generals valued greatly. As Rossignol proved his worth again and again, he was showered with privilege and wealth. On his deathbed, Louis XIII told his queen that Rossignol was one of the men most necessary to the good of the state.

Antoine Rossignol
M.^e des Comptes.

The high regard in which Rossignol was clearly held secured him a place in the court of Louis' successor, the 'Sun King' Louis XIV, where the cryptographer's wealth only increased.

CODEMAKING FATHER AND SON

In fact, Antoine's son, Bonaventure, also rose to prominence as a cryptographer, and together they invented the 'great cipher', a kind of enhanced monoalphabetic cipher that was particularly resistant to cracking.

The cipher performed substitutions on syllables rather than individual letters, and included a host of tricks, including a codegroup that meant 'ignore the preceding codegroup'.

The great cipher was used to encrypt the king's most secret messages for some time, but after the death of Antoine and Bonaventure Rossignol, the cipher fell out of use and the precise details of its system were lost. Such was its strength against cracking, the cipher remained unbroken for many generations, which in turn meant that much enciphered correspondence in the royal archives was unreadable.

That was the case until 1890, when a new series of letters written using the great cipher were passed to another renowned French cryptanalyst, commandant Étienne Bazeries, who spent three hard years working on a solution.

Eventually, he recognised the nature of the cipher when he guessed that a particular sequence of repeated numbers, 124-22-125-46-345, stood for 'les ennemis' (*the enemies*). From that snippet of a clue he was able to unravel the entire cipher.

Incidentally, historians also remember Bazeries as the inventor of his own cylindrical device for encryption, which had 20 rotors, each with 25 alphabet letters. The system was rejected by the French military, although the US army adopted it in 1922.

The great successes of the Rossignols made it patently clear to the rulers of France that the interception of enciphered messages from rival powers had great value. At the urging of the father and son team,

Opposite: Antoine Rossignol (1600–1682), one of the great names of cryptography, whose son and grandson continued the tradition.

the country established one of the first dedicated branches of the public service to perform this task.

Called the **Cabinet Noir** (black chamber), a French team of codebreakers was routinely intercepting and reading the dispatches of foreign diplomats from the 1700s onward.

What's more, this institutionalised cryptanalysis became common practice across Europe in the eighteenth century. Undoubtedly the most famous of them all was the one that operated in Vienna – the **Geheime Kabinets-Kanzlei** (which translates roughly as Secret Legal Office).

The Viennese black chamber was founded during the rule of Empress Maria Theresa, the only female ruler in the Habsburg dynasty's 650-year history, and was renowned for its fantastic efficiency. It needed to be. Vienna was one of Europe's commercial and diplomatic crossroads during the 1700s, with large amounts of mail passing through the city's post offices on a daily basis. The black chamber made the most of that activity. Each bag of mail due to be delivered to local embassies was first brought to the black chamber, at about seven in the morning, where staff would read and copy out the important parts, reseal the letters and send them on their way for delivery by 9:30. Mail simply passing through the city would be dealt with in a similar way – if more slowly.

Any encrypted messages would be subjected to skilled analysis – the Viennese cabinet had a fully fledged training scheme in operation for apprentice cryptanalysts, which ensured a steady supply of well-educated professionals to keep the Empress ahead of the game.

Meanwhile, Britain also had its own form of institutionalised cryptanalysis – the cunningly named **Deciphering Branch**. This government agency was also a kind of family business, dominated as it was by the churchman Edward Willes, later Bishop of St. David's, and his sons.

The Willes men and their fellow 'decypherers' were sent intercepted letters by the Secret Office and the Private Office, two spying divisions of the Post Office. Thanks to their work, the British king and government learned of machinations in France, Austria, Spain, Portugal and elsewhere. Knowledge filtered out of encrypted

The descent of the French army on St. John's, Newfoundland, 1762, during the Seven Years' War. Through the newly formed 'Deciphering Branch,' the British were able to intercept vital information during the war.

letters by England's decipherers helped the government learn, for example, that Spain had allied with France against England in the Seven Years' War.

But the routine letter opening wasn't limited to messages from overseas. Politicians were soon finding that their own correspondence was being monitored. In the late nineteenth century, Herbert Joyce wrote in his book, *The History of the Post Office*, that:

'As early as 1735 Members of Parliament had begun to complain that their letters bore evident signs of having been opened at the Post Office, alleging that such opening had become frequent and was becoming a matter of common notoriety … it transpired that in the Post Office there was a private office, an office independent of the Postmaster-General and under the immediate direction of the Secretary of State, which was expressly maintained for the purpose of opening and inspecting letters. It was pretended, indeed, that these operations were confined to foreign letters, but, in the matter of fact, there was no such restriction… it was in June 1742 that these shameful facts became known through the report of a committee of the House of Commons.'

Overall, the skilled work of the black chambers increased the pressure on cryptographers to use polyalphabetic ciphers like Vigenère's. That pressure would soon be magnified many times by technological advances. With the dawning of the era of electrical communication, everything was about to change once again.

THE MAN IN THE IRON MASK

TOUJOURS SEUL!!!
ou
LE MASQUE DE FER

PAROLES DE
E. BARATEAU.   MUSIQUE DE
AD. BOÏELDIEU.

Nº1 Tenor ou Soprano   Nº2 Baryton ou Contralto.
PARIS.
J. B. Jamard, Editeur

Like many great mysteries, the tale of the Man in the Iron Mask has fascinated artists for centuries. Poets, novelists and movie directors have probed the true identity of the unknown man who was imprisoned in France in the dying years of the seventeenth century. The tale also inspired one of the more notable feats in the history of cryptanalysis.

It all began in 1698, when a mysterious man was imprisoned in the Bastille. He had been a captive of the French government since 1687 or earlier, but for all that time his face had been obscured by a mask. Nobody seemed to know who he was, where he had come from or what his crime was; only that this was his punishment.

The writer and philosopher Voltaire was among the first to record the tale of this mysterious individual in his book *Siècle de Louis* XIV. He recorded that a man who had never been seen, except when his face was hidden by an iron mask, was transferred to the prison from the island of Sainte-Marguerite – having previously been in the fortress of Pignerol – and died there in 1703 at about the age of 60.

Voltaire himself had been imprisoned for a year in the Bastille in 1717, and during his incarceration apparently spoke to several people who had served the Man in the Iron Mask. He was reported to be young, tall and handsome, dressing in lace and linen finery.

Voltaire dropped some broad hints that the man was the brother of Louis XIV – pointing out that he was the same age as the king, and bore a striking resemblance to someone famous. Alexander Dumas, in his novel, suggested much the same, and this myth is the one that has persisted, in spite of some striking evidence unearthed in the nineteenth century by the skilled cryptologist Étienne Bazeries.

When Bazeries cracked the Great Cipher of Louis XIV by uncovering the fact that the numeric cipher groups related to syllables of text, he suddenly laid bare many secrets. A trove of high-level correspondence from the royal court could then be deciphered.

One day, he solved a dispatch from July of 1691, which described how the king was deeply

Opposite and above: The drama of the story has captured the imagination of playwrights and film-makers alike.

unhappy with a commander who had lifted the siege of a northern Italian town, resulting in a defeat for the French army.

The dispatch ordered that the man responsible for the defeat, Vivien Labbé, Seigneur du Bulonde, be arrested and that troops should 'conduct him to the fortress of Pignerol, where His Majesty desires that he be guarded locked in a cell of that fortress at night and having the liberty during the day of walking on the battlements with a 330 309'.

These two cipher groups at the end of the message didn't appear anywhere else in the dispatches – so Bazeries made a leap of faith and decided that they had to stand for the word 'masque' and a full-stop.

Despite this great leap, Bazeries announced that Bulonde was indeed the Man in the Mask.

Is the letter a false trail? Does 330 309 really mean masque? What about suggestions that Bulonde was still alive in 1703? Other candidates for the role of Man in the Iron Mask include the Duc de Beaufort and the Comte de Vermandois, natural son of Louis XIV. Writer John Noone, in his 1998 book *The Man Behind the Iron Mask*, suggests it was simply an unlucky valet who was kept in a mask to boost the fearsome reputation of his jailor.

It seems Bazeries took a leap too far. Perhaps the identity of the Man in the Iron Mask is one of those secrets that will continue to baffle, and inspire, for some time to come.

CHAPTER THREE

WIT

Technology triggered more cryptology revolutions,
but plenty of ciphers remain unsolved.
Digraphs, Playfair and Elgar's other Enigma.

Another major upheaval was waiting for the field of cryptology in the middle of the nineteenth century. This time, the impetus was the birth of a new type of communication technology that forced cryptographers to seek new ways to keep the messages secret.

The revolution was sparked in 1844, when the American inventor Samuel Morse built his first telegraph line, stretching a distance of nearly 60 km (40 miles) between Baltimore, Maryland and Washington, DC. On 24 May of that year, Morse sent a famously Biblical telegram – 'What hath God wrought' – from the Supreme Court room in Washington to his assistant, Alfred Vail, in Baltimore.

In Morse Code, the message would have been transmitted as shown below:

.− − .....− − .....− − ....− − .− − − − ...− − .− .− − − ..− − − .....−

In sending the message, Morse demonstrated to the world that long-distance electric communication was possible, and jump-started a revolution that would have an enormous impact on society.

Before long, businessmen began to apply the technology to make almost instantaneous deals, newspapers took advantage of its speed to gather news more quickly and government ministries used it for

Opposite: Samuel Morse (1791–1972), inventor of the Morse Code.

domestic and international communication. Within a few decades, a
network of telegraph cables had traversed oceans to all the continents
on the globe, making instant worldwide communication a reality.

But for all its speed, the telegraph had one perceived downside – a
decided lack of security. Morse had invented a system of short and
long pulses for sending messages through his system, called Morse
Code, but its code-book was in the public domain so it was useless for
keeping secrets.

In 1853, an article in the English publication *Quarterly Review*
illustrated the problem:

> *Means should also be undertaken to obviate one great objection,
> at present felt with respect to sending private communications by
> telegraph – the violation of all secrecy – for in any case half-a-
> dozen people must be cognisant of every word addressed by one
> person to another.*

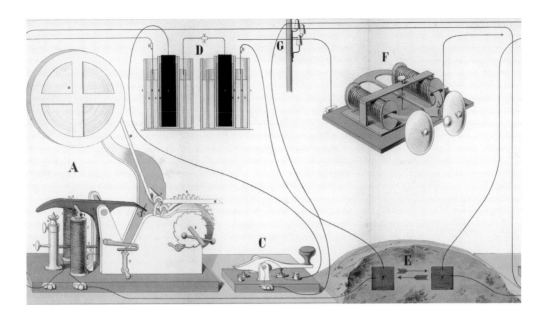

The trouble was that telegraph clerks had to read the message in order to transmit it. Awareness of this problem inspired dozens of people to think up their own supposedly 'unbreakable' ciphers. The plaintext message would be encrypted using one or another method, and the transformed text would then be turned into the dots and dashes of Morse code by a telegraph operator oblivious to the true meaning of the message. Soon, scores of private cryptosystems had evolved to fill this need, many of them developed by amateurs.

The military also adapted to the new technology. For tactical messages, codes or nomenclators were abandoned as being too hard to reissue to scores of telegraph stations. Soon enough, important military messages were being encrypted using the old polyalphabetic Vigenère cipher, the 'unbreakable' *chiffre indéchiffrable*.

Thus, the telegraph is credited with revolutionising cryptography. Not only did it allow encrypted messages to be delivered at once across thousands of miles, but it also ensured that after 450 years in which codes and nomenclators had dominated, the neglected art of the cipher was back in fashion.

LOVE AFFAIRS AND
LITERARY CIPHERS

The telegraph encouraged generals, diplomats and businessmen to use cryptography as a way of ensuring the secrecy of their telegrams. But the new fascination with cryptography wasn't limited to grand affairs of state or commerce.

Around the same time, ordinary men and women also became more comfortable with the idea of ciphers and would use encryption to ensure their personal messages were only read by their intended recipients.

The fascination also extended beyond the telegram. In newspapers, young lovers of the late Victorian era would submit encrypted messages to the personals columns – known as 'agony columns' in recognition of their writers' amorous suffering – as a way of conducting their romance away from the disapproving eyes of parents and others.

The codes and ciphers these tortured romantics used were generally fairly simple, and amateur cryptanalysts made a game out of breaking the messages and revealing their saucy contents.

For example, the famous cryptologists Charles Wheatstone, Fellow of the Royal Society, and Lyon Playfair, first Baron Playfair of St Andrews, liked decrypting these messages as a bit of Sunday afternoon fun. Walking together across London's Hammersmith Bridge, the two friends – both short and bespectacled – would work through the personals columns in *The Times* of London. On one occasion, Wheatstone and Playfair unravelled the messages being sent between an Oxford student and his sweetheart. When the student suggested elopement, Wheatstone took matters into his own hands, placing an advertisement of his own in the couple's cipher, urging them to abandon their foolhardy plan. Soon there followed another message: Dear Charlie: Write no more. Our cipher is discovered!

The public's growing interest in cryptography spilled over into literature, too. Several of the nineteenth century's most well-known writers wove cryptographic techniques into their novels.

William Makepeace Thackeray, for example, made use of a steganographic technique in his 1852 work *The History of Henry Osmond*. The technique he used is known as a Cardano grille, attributed to an Italian doctor of the sixteenth century. In it, several rectangular pieces, the height of a line of text, are cut out of a stiff piece of paper or card.

To encipher a message with a Cardano grille, one puts the cardboard with the slots cut in it over a blank piece of paper and writes in the ciphertext. Then remove the grille and fill in the rest of the page with innocuous sounding text. To reveal the message, put a grille of the same design over the top of the paper to reveal the hidden message. Devices such as these were used as recently as World War II.

Left: Girolamo Cardano (1501–1576), Italian mathematician and scholar, and inventor of the Cardano grille.

THE INGENIOUS PROFESSOR BABBAGE

Above: Charles Babbage (1792–1871).
Opposite top: Analytical Engine of 1834.
Opposite bottom: A newspaper boy holding a placard
for the *Pall Mall Gazette* of Saturday 21 October 1871.
The placard contains the headlines of the day, including
the 'Death of Mr Babbage'.

Charles Babbage, English eccentric and inventor,
is without doubt the most fascinating figure
among all those who dabbled in cryptology in the
nineteenth century.

Babbage had a remarkable mind. Not only is
he remembered as the man who invented
standard postage rates, and compiled the first
reliable actuarial tables, he also invented a kind of
speedometer and discovered that the width of tree
rings depends on that year's weather.

But he is most famous for his role as one of the
fathers of mechanical computing. In his
autobiography, he remembered an occasion in
1812 when he was sitting in the rooms of the
Analytical Society, at Cambridge, daydreaming
over a table of logarithms that was lying open
before him. 'Another member, coming into the
room, and seeing me half asleep, called out,
"Well, Babbage, what are you dreaming about?"
to which I replied, 'I am thinking that all these
tables' (pointing to the logarithms) 'might be
calculated by machinery.'

By the early 1820s he had conceived a plan to
build a machine that could calculate such tables
to a high degree of accuracy. He called the
machine his 'Difference Engine', and figured
that it would require 25,000 parts with a total
weight of 15 tons. But despite receiving some
£17,000 funding from the government, and
investing thousands of his own in the project, it
was never completed.

Around the same time that work on the
Difference Engine stopped, Babbage developed
an even more remarkable idea – an 'Analytical
Engine', which would be capable of solving a
variety of problems. He tinkered with ideas for
this forerunner of programmable computers
until his death in 1871.

Babbage had been born in 1792, and his
fascination with mathematics seems to have arisen
early during a sickly childhood. He also developed
an early interest in cryptanalysis, a hobby that he

recalled later would sometimes provoke the violent displeasure of his older schoolmates: 'The bigger boys made ciphers, but if I got hold of a few words, I usually found out the key,' he wrote. 'The consequence of this ingenuity was occasionally painful: the owners of the detected ciphers sometimes thrashed me, though the fault lay in their own stupidity.'

The beatings didn't dissuade him from an interest in the field, however, and as an adult he seems to have become something of a society cryptanalyst. In 1850, for example, he solved a cipher of the wife of King Charles I, Henrietta Maria, and also helped a biographer by solving a note written in shorthand by England's first Astronomer Royal, John Flamsteed. In 1854, a barrister sought his help in solving some cryptic letters needed for evidence in a case.

Like his contemporaries Wheatstone and Playfair, Babbage was also fond of solving the enciphered notices in the newspaper agony columns, but his interest was far from limited to cracking easy ciphers. In fact, he is now known to have been capable of deciphering supposedly uncrackable polyalphabetic ciphers.

Babbage's mammoth achievement wasn't fully appreciated until modern times, however. Like so many of the ideas he dreamed up, his crypto-logical work went largely unpublished. Some have suggested that the work was kept secret at the insistence of British intelligence services, who used it to break the communications of their military foes.

Meanwhile, in Prussia, a retired army officer by the name of Friedrich Kasiski was working out his own techniques for cracking polyalphabetic ciphers with repeating keys.

In 1863, Kasiski published a short but momentous book on cryptology, entitled *Die Geheimschriften und die Dechiffrierkunst* ('Secret Writing and the Art of Deciphering'), in which he outlined a general means of solving the types of ciphers that had baffled cryptanalysts for centuries. Kasiski's 95-page volume advised cryptanalysts who were faced with a suspected polyalphabetic cipher to 'calculate the distance separating the repetitions from one another ... and endeavour to break up this number into its factors ... The factor most frequently found indicates the number of letters in the key'.

Babbage is also now remembered as the man who came up with the first ever solution of Vigenère's formidable **autokey** cipher, in which the plaintext message is incorporated into the key. To write a message using an autokey, you can start the key with a short keyword, and then follow it with the text of your message. The benefits of this system are that the sender and receiver of the message both need only know the short priming keyword, and it avoids the weaknesses of a cipher with a repeating keyword.

Imagine you want to send a message 'begin the attack at dawn', and decide that your keyword will be rosemary. The key then becomes 'rosemarybegintheattackatdawn'. As with other encipherments using Vigenère's table, the top row is used to locate the plaintext letter. Run your finger down that column until you reach the row beginning with the key letter.

For key **r** and plaintext **b**, the ciphertext is **S**, found at the intersection of row **r** and column **b**.

The beginning of the encryption process will look like this:

Key	r	o	s	e	m	a	r	y	b	e	g	i	n	t	h	e	a	t	t	a
Plaintext	b	e	g	i	n	t	h	e	a	t	t	a	c	k	a	t	d	a	w	n
ciphertext	S	S	Y	M	Z	T	Y	C	B	X	Z	I	P	D	H	X	D	T	P	N

This gives the ciphertext as SSYMZTYCBXZIPDHXDTPN

For the intended recipient of the message (or anyone who knows the keyword rosemary), deciphering the message is a straightforward process. First, decipher the plaintext letters that have been encrypted using the word rosemary. Do this by finding where the ciphertext letter appears in the rows beginning with each of the keyword letters. For the first letter, for example, look along the row beginning with **r** and find the letter **S**. Look up the column to find what plaintext letter is at its top – in this case, **b**.

Once you've unscrambled the section of ciphertext corresponding to 'rosemary', you will have the first part of the message 'begin the'. Now, you use those eight letters as the key to decipher the next eight letters of ciphertext. Keep repeating this process until the message is solved.

Figuring out the length of the key is a crucial development because it allows the cryptanalyst to line up the ciphertext in the same number of columns as there are letters in the key.

Each of these columns can then be treated as the ciphertext of a monoalphabetic cipher. Instead of trying to decipher a message that has been encrypted with an unknown number of different cipher alphabets, suddenly you are in a position to know which letters in the ciphertext were encrypted using the same cipher alphabet. By grouping those letters together, you can subject them to frequency analysis and the other tricks used to crack monoalphabetic ciphers. This procedure came to be known as the **Kasiski examination**.

Take the following ciphertext, for example. It is taken from a US military field manual on ciphers.

FNPDM GJRMF FTFFZ IQKTC LGHAS EOSIM PVLZF LJEWU WTEAH
EOZUA NBHNJ SXFFT JNRGR KOEXP GZSEY XHNFS EZAGU EORHZ
XOMRH ZBLTF BYQDT DAKEI LKSIP UYKSX BTERQ QTWPI SAOSF
TQKTS QLZVE EYVAW JSNFB IFNEI OZJNR RFSPR TWHNJ ROJSI
UOCZB GQPLI STUAE KSSQT EFXUJ NFGKO UHLZF HPRYV TUSCP
JDJSE BLSYU IXDSJ JAEVF KJNQF FIFMP EHYQD

Step one is to look for repeated sequences of letters, ideally three or more letters long. They are underlined in the text above. Next, analyse how far apart the repeated sequences are, counting from the beginning of the first sequence until the letter before the next occurrence.

Next, you need to calculate the possible factors for those distances.

Repeats	Distance	Possible factors
FFT	48 characters	3, 4, 6, 8, 12
QKT	120	3, 4, 5, 6, 8, 10, 12
LZF	180	3, 4, 6, 10, 12, 15
HNJ	12	3, 4, 5, 6, 8, 10, 12
JNR	102	3, 6
RHZ	6	3, 6

The only factors common to all the repeated sequences is 6, so the next step is to write out the ciphertext in six columns. Each of the columns of text is assumed to have been encrypted using one cipher alphabet.

1	2	3	4	5	6
F	N	P	D	M	G
J	R	M	F	F	T
F	F	Z	I	Q	K
T	C	L	G	H	A
S	E	O	S	I	M
P	V	L	Z	F	L
J	E	W	U	W	T
E	A	H	E	O	Z
U	A	N	B	H	N
J	S	X	F	F	T
J	N	R	G	R	K
O	E	X	P	G	Z
S	E	Y	X	H	N
F	S	E	Z	A	G
U	E	O	R	H	Z
X	O	M	R	H	Z
B	L	T	F	B	Y
Q	D	T	D	A	K
E	I	L	K	S	I
P	U	Y	K	S	X
B	T	E	R	Q	Q
T	W	P	I	S	A
O	S	F	T	Q	K
T	S	Q	L	Z	V
E	E	Y	V	A	W
J	S	N	F	B	I
F	N	E	I	O	Z
J	N	R	R	F	S
P	R	T	W	H	N
J	R	O	J	S	I
U	O	C	Z	B	G
Q	P	L	I	S	T
U	A	E	K	S	S
Q	T	E	F	X	U
J	N	F	G	K	O
U	H	L	Z	F	H
P	R	Y	V	T	U
S	C	P	J	D	J
S	E	B	L	S	Y
U	I	X	D	S	J
J	A	E	V	F	K
J	N	Q	F	F	I
F	M	P	E	H	Y
Q	D				

Now we can do a frequency count for letters in each column. For column one we get the following.

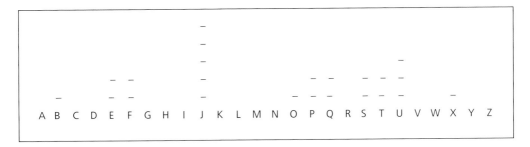

For the cryptanalyst, this frequency distribution contains a few clues. Perhaps **J**, the most common letter, is substituted for **e**? On the other hand, there are distinct clusters of high frequency letters at **OPQ** and **STU**, so perhaps they represent **nop** and **rst** – part of the normal pattern of distribution – in plaintext English. If so, ciphertext **B** would represent plaintext **A**, and so on.

When you repeat the process for column two, you get a different picture:

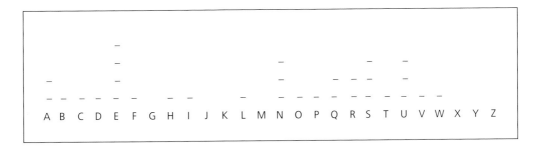

This pattern is highly reminiscent of the normal frequencies of letters. Perhaps in these letters, plaintext and ciphertext are the same?

Once you start to make guesses about the encryptions performed on each letter in the ciphertext, you can start substituting letters back in to see if they make sense.

So far, we have reason to suspect that the letters in the first column have undergone a shift of one place and that those in the second have not been changed at all. If we also calculate that the fifth column has undergone a shift of 14 places, fragments of words begin to appear. For example, the first few letters are 'en__y', which perhaps is part of the word 'enemy'.

If the first word of the plaintext is indeed 'enemy', that would mean the third column of text has been shifted 11 places (from **e** to **P**) and that the fourth column has been shifted 17 places (from **m** to **D**). We can test whether these guesses are correct by trying the same shift on the next few letters in the ciphertext. This would give us a partial plaintext of 'enemy_ irbor_ eforc_ ' (see below), which would seem to make sense as part of the phrase 'enemy airborne force'. In turn, this suggests that the first plaintext letter in column 6 is **a**, perhaps having undergone a shift of six places to **G**. In this way, a solution can be pieced together step by step.

1	2	3	4	5	6
e	n			y	
F	N	P	D	M	G
i	r			r	
J	R	M	F	F	T
e	f		c		
K	F	Z	I	Q	K
s	c		t		
T	C	L	G	H	A
r	e			u	
S	E	O	S	I	M
o	v		r		
P	V	L	Z	F	L
l	e	i		i	
J	E	W	U	W	T
d	a			a	
E	A	H	E	O	Z
t	a		t		
U	A	N	B	H	N
l	s		r		
J	S	X	F	F	T
l	n		d		
J	N	R	G	R	K
n	e		s		
O	E	X	P	G	Z
r	e		t		
S	E	Y	X	H	N
e	s		m		
F	S	E	Z	A	G

Our guesswork so far suggests that the text was enciphered using a Vigenère cipher with the keyword **BALROG**. We can now make use of a tableau to speed up the deciphering (see below).

The six different alphabets used to encipher the message have been written out, each one beginning with the relevant letter of the keyword. For the first letter of the message, use the first alphabet. Read along that row until you find the ciphertext **F**, then read up to get the plaintext letter at the top of the column, in this case **e**. Carry on in this way, moving down to the second alphabet to decipher the second letter of ciphertext, the third alphabet for the third letter and so on. For the seventh letter, go back to alphabet 1.

	a	b	c	d	e	f	g	h	i	j	k	l	m	n	o	p	q	r	s	t	u	v	w	x	y	z
1	B	C	D	E	F	G	H	I	J	K	L	M	N	O	P	Q	R	S	T	U	V	W	X	Y	Z	A
2	A	B	C	D	E	F	G	H	I	J	K	L	M	N	O	P	Q	R	S	T	U	V	W	X	Y	Z
3	L	M	N	O	P	Q	R	S	T	U	V	W	X	Y	Z	A	B	C	D	E	F	G	H	I	J	K
4	R	S	T	U	V	W	X	Y	Z	A	B	C	D	E	F	G	H	I	J	K	L	M	N	O	P	Q
5	O	P	Q	R	S	T	U	V	W	X	Y	Z	A	B	C	D	E	F	G	H	I	J	K	L	M	N
6	G	H	I	J	K	L	M	N	O	P	Q	R	S	T	U	V	W	X	Y	Z	A	B	C	D	E	F

The full plaintext is therefore revealed as:

'enemy airborne forces captured bugov airfield in dawn attack this morning pd enemy strength estimated at two battalions pd immediate counter attacks were unsuccessful pd enemy is concentrating armor in third sector in apparent attempt to join up with airborne forces pd request immediate reinforcements pd.'

(pd in this example stands for period, marking the end of a sentence.)

THE PLAYFAIR CIPHER

In the early weeks of 1854, Lyon Playfair, a Scottish scientist and parliamentarian, was a guest at a high society dinner that had been arranged by Lord Granville, president of the governing council.

In the course of the evening, Playfair described to his fellow guests a new type of cipher that his friend Charles Wheatstone had designed as a means of making telegraph communications secure.

The cipher was the first to use a digraph substitution, in which letters are substituted on a two-by-two basis rather than individually.

To use the cipher, first choose a keyword that sender and receiver of the message both know – say, for example, SQUARE. In a 5 x 5 square, write out the key (omitting any repetition of letters), followed by the remaining letters of the alphabet in order, and combining I and J into a single unit:

S	Q	U	A	R
E	B	C	D	F
G	H	IJ	K	L
M	N	O	P	T
V	W	X	Y	Z

To encipher your message, divide the plaintext into pairs. Any double letters need to be separated by an *x*, and an *x* is added to make a final single letter into a digraph. So the word *common* would become *co mx mo nx*.

Once the letters are divided into pairs, each two-letter digraph falls into one of three categories. Either both letters are in the same row, both are in the same column or neither.

Letters that are in the same row are each replaced with the letter to their right in the square – so, np would become OT. Each row is treated as cyclical, so that the letter to the 'right' of r in the square above is S, for example.

Letters that appear in the same column are replaced by the letter directly beneath it by the same method.

In the case of plaintext letters that appear in neither the same row nor the same column, each one is replaced by the letter that lies in its own row, and the column occupied by the other letter. So, ep would become DM.

To decipher digraphic ciphers like Playfair's, one approach is to look for the most common digraphs in the ciphertext and assume they represent the most frequent digraphs in the language you think the plaintext is written in. In English, these are th, he, an, in, er, re and es.

Another trick is to look for reversed digraphs in the ciphertext, such as BF and FB. In text enciphered using Playfair, these will always decrypt to the same letter pattern in the plaintext, for example DE and ED.

The cryptanalyst might have success by looking for nearby reversed digraphs in the ciphertext and matching the pattern to known

Above: Lyon Playfair, Baron of St Andrews (1818–1898).

plaintext words containing the pattern, like REvERsed or DEfeatED, as a way to start reconstructing the key.

Wheatstone and Playfair took the cipher to the Under Secretary of the Foreign Office, but he considered the system too complicated. Wheatstone countered that he only needed 15 minutes and he could teach the technique to three out of four boys in the nearest elementary school. 'That is very possible,' the Under Secretary replied, 'but you could never teach it to attachés.'

Eventually, in spite of this initial scepticism, the British War Office did take up the cipher. Although it had been invented by Wheatstone, the cipher has always been known by the name of the man who lobbied the UK government to take it up, Playfair.

CIPHERS IN THE AMERICAN CIVIL WAR

On 12 April 12 1861, the Confederate General P. G. T. Beauregard opened fire upon Fort Sumter in Charleston, South Carolina, and began the American Civil War. Soon thereafter, the governor of Ohio summoned to the state capital a 36-year-old telegrapher by the name of Anson Stager.

The governor knew that the outbreak of war had made secure telegraphic communications essential, and he had two requests for Stager: develop a system so the governor could securely communicate over the telegraph with the governors of Illinois and Indiana, and assume control of the Ohio Military District's telegraph lines.

Stager was a good choice. He had been 19 years old when Samuel Morse had brought the telegraph into existence in 1844. An apprentice printer for Henry O'Reilly of Rochester, New York, Stager had hoped to work in the printing business; instead, in 1846, he was introduced to the telegraph.

O'Reilly constructed a telegraph line in Pennsylvania, and Stager was placed in charge at one of the stations. As the O'Reilly telegraph lines expanded, so did Stager's responsibilities. He moved to Ohio to manage telegraph lines there and eventually served as the first general superintendent of Western Union Telegraph Company, newly formed in 1856.

In response to the governor's request, Stager developed a simple and effective cipher system. Soon, word of its benefits had reached the Union's Major-General George B. McClellan, who then asked Stager to come up with a military cipher along the same lines.

Within a short time, Stager's cipher had gained widespread acceptance throughout the Union forces, and its simplicity and dependability meant it was the most widely-used cipher during the Civil War.

In essence it was based on **word transposition**, or rearrangement of the order of the words in a message. The plaintext of the message was written out in lines, and the words then transcribed by column. The use of ordinary words, rather than groups of incoherent letters, made it less susceptible to errors.

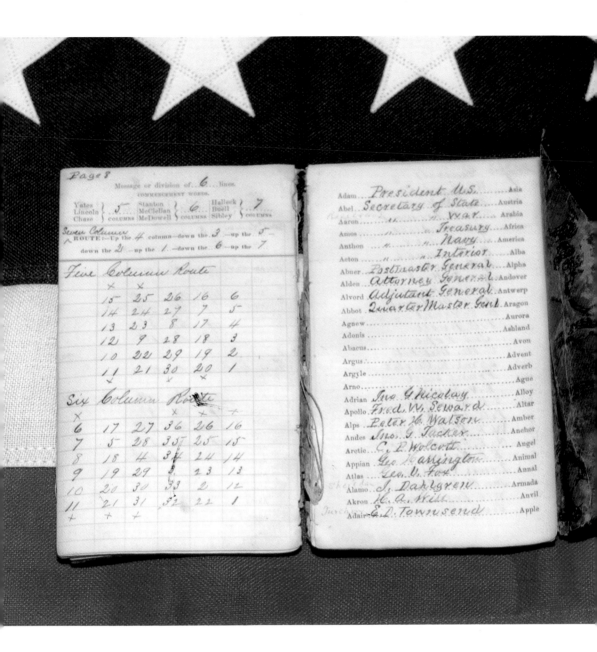

As the war progressed, Stager and the Union cipher operators developed variations on the **Union route cipher** – ten in all – in which different selections of code words were used to replace words in messages, and in which different routes were chosen to weave up and down the columns of text.

Above: Codebook used in the Civil War.

Here's an example of how the system worked, based on a message sent by Abraham Lincoln in the middle of 1863. The message plaintext read as follows:

For Colonel Ludlow.
Richardson and Brown, correspondents of the Tribune, captured at Vicksburg, are detained at Richmond. Please ascertain why they are detained and get them off if you can. The President. 4.30 p.m.

The code system that was in use at the time replaced VENUS for colonel, WAYLAND for captured, ODOR for Vicksburg, NEPTUNE for Richmond, ADAM for President of US and NELLY for 4.30 p.m.

Substituting those words renders the message like this:

For VENUS Ludlow
Richardson and Brown, Correspondents of the Tribune, WAYLAND at ODOR, are detained at NEPTUNE. Please ascertain why they are detained and get them off if you can. ADAM, NELLY

To encipher the message, the cipher operator chose a route. In this case he chose GUARD, which required that the message be written out in seven lines of five words with 'nulls', or meaningless words, added to complete the rectangle. In this table, the words of the plaintext message are in lower case, while the codewords are in capitals:

For	VENUS	Ludlow	Richardson	And
Brown	Correspondents	Of	The	Tribune
Wayland	At	ODOR	Are	Detained
At	NEPTUNE	Please	Ascertain	Why
They	Are	Detained	And	Get
Them	Off	If	You	Can
ADAM	NELLY	THIS	FILLS	UP

To transpose the words, in this case, the encipherer read up the first column, down the second, up the fifth, down the fourth and finally up the third. To add further to the security, another meaningless 'null' word was added at the end of each column.

GUARD ADAM THEM THEY AT WAYLAND BROWN FOR						KISSING
VENUS CORRESPONDENTS AT NEPTUNE ARE OFF NELLY						TURNING
UP CAN GET WHY DETAINED TRIBUNE AND						TIMES
RICHARDSON THE ARE ASCERTAIN AND YOU FILLS						BELLY
THIS IF DETAINED PLEASE ODOR OF LUDLO						COMMISSIONER

This gave the final message as:

GUARD ADAM THEM THEY AT WAYLAND BROWN FOR KISSING VENUS CORRESPONDENTS AT NEPTUNE ARE OFF NELLY TURNING UP CAN GET WHY DETAINED TRIBUNE AND TIMES RICHARDSON THE ARE ASCERTAIN AND YOU FILLS BELLY THIS IF DETAINED PLEASE ODOR OF LUDLOW COMMISSIONER

The Fall of Vicksburg in Mississippi to Union troops, 1863.

HIDDEN TREASURE, HIDDEN MEANING –
THE BEALE PAPERS

For many of those who became fascinated with cryptography in the nineteenth century, the joy and satisfaction of cracking a code might have been reward enough for their efforts. But if that wasn't quite satisfying, perhaps $30 million of buried treasure was more of an incentive.

That was the pot of gold waiting at the end of a cryptological rainbow known as The Beale Papers, a mystery that surfaced in 1885 when a man named J. B. Ward began selling a pamphlet about a treasure trove hidden in the state of Virginia. Ward's pamphlet described the tale of one Thomas Jefferson Beale and the encrypted message he had supposedly left at the Washington Hotel in Lynchburg, Virginia, USA, in the 1820s.

Beale, the pamphlet said, had visited the hotel for the first time in January 1820, staying for the winter and bringing himself to the attention of the hotel owner, Robert Morriss, who thought him 'the handsomest man I had ever seen'. He left abruptly in March, and returned two years later, once again spending the rest of the winter in Lynchburg. This time, before he left he entrusted Morriss with a locked iron box that he said contained 'papers of value and importance'.

The pamphlet explained that Morriss guarded the box faithfully for 23 years until, in 1845, he broke into it. The note inside described how in April 1817 Beale and 29 others had journeyed across America, through the Western plains to Santa Fe, before heading north. In a small ravine, according to the note, the posse struck it lucky – 'discovering a large quantity of gold in a cleft in the rocks'.

A decision was made to hide the riches in a secret location in Virginia, first trading some of the heavy gold for jewels. This was the task that brought Beale to Lynchburg in 1820. Apparently, the subsequent visit was made because the group was worried that, in case of an accident, the treasure would not find its way to their relatives.

Beale's job was to find a reliable person, who could be confided in to carry out their wishes in the event of their sudden death, and he chose Morriss. After reading the note, Morriss felt obliged to pass the note on to the relatives of the men, but he was stuck – the description of the treasure, its location and the names of the relatives had been encrypted into three sheets of meaningless numbers. The note supposedly said the key to the cipher would be posted by a third party. It never arrived.

According to the pamphlet, the story goes that in 1862, nearing the end of his life, Morriss confided his secret to a friend – Ward – who made a stunningly intuitive breakthrough in deciphering the second of the three encrypted pages. Apparently, he guessed that the numbers in the sequence corresponded with words in the Declaration of Independence. So, the number 73 stands for the 73rd word in the declaration – which is 'hold' – and so on.

Continuing this process, the pamphleteer revealed the following message from Beale:

'I have deposited in the county of Bedford, about four miles from Buford's, in an excavation or vault, six feet below the surface of the ground, the following articles: … The deposit consists of two

Above: The Declaration of Independence.

thousand nine hundred and twenty one pounds of gold and five thousand one hundred pounds of silver; also jewels, obtained in St. Louis in exchange for silver to save transportation … The above is securely packed in iron pots, with iron covers. The vault is roughly lined with stone, and the vessels rest on solid stone, and are covered with others …'

Unfortunately, using the Declaration of Independence as a key failed to unlock the other two Beale ciphers, Ward wrote in his pamphlet.

Generations of codebreakers have also failed to unlock the secret of the Beale Papers – including some of the brightest cryptanalytic minds in the USA. Sceptics have little hesitation in pronouncing the pamphlet a hoax, but for some the temptation of immense wealth combined with a code challenge that has thwarted so many for so long is too great to resist.

In the twentieth century, the giant of US cryptography, William Friedman, was disparaging about the lack of sophistication in the Union system. Yet it proved remarkably effective, and the Confederate forces never managed to solve the Union's encrypted messages.

The Confederates themselves, however, never achieved the same level of security. The rebels often used the Vigenère cipher, but transmission errors caused no end of trouble.

The security of Confederate communications was also under threat from a trio of young cipher operators working in the War Department building next to the White House. These three men – David Homer Bates, Charles A. Tinker and Albert B. Chandler – grew used to the sight of Lincoln crossing the lawn in the direction of their office and coming into the room to read through specially prepared carbon copies of messages.

The three men, barely out of their teens, broke several Confederate cryptograms during the course of the war, including letters between rebels plotting to print bonds and money for use by the Confederacy.

THE MIGHTY KERCKHOFFS

One man the Confederates might have found very useful in their efforts to crack the Union army's ciphers was Auguste Kerckhoffs, a schoolteacher who lived, around the time of the American Civil War, in the French town of Melun, some 25 miles outside Paris.

Kerckhoffs was a skilled linguist with a wide range of interests. After spending much of his working life teaching in high schools and universities, in 1883 he wrote a book that had an enormous impact on cryptology in France and beyond.

Kerckhoffs' book, *La Cryptographie Militaire*, was originally published as a pair of essays in the French *Journal of Military Science*. In them, he cast a critical eye over the state of the art of cryptography and urged the need for improvements in the way the French did things. In particular, he was concerned with finding a solution to the major cryptographic problem of the age – finding a confidential system that was also accessible and simple enough to use, suitable for use via the telegraph.

In the first of the essays, he set out a list of six dictums that remain to this day a benchmark for those who are developing field ciphers. According to Kerckhoffs, the requirements of a military cipher can be boiled down to the following:

1 The system must be substantially, if not mathematically, undecipherable;
2 The system must not require secrecy and can be stolen by the enemy without causing trouble;
3 It must be easy to communicate and remember the keys without requiring written notes; it must also be easy to change or modify the keys with different participants;
4 The system ought to be compatible with telegraph communication;
5 The system must be portable, and its use must not require more than one person;
6 The system must be easy to use and must neither require stress of mind nor the knowledge of a long series of rules.

Of these six rules, the most famous is the second, which implies that a cryptosystem should be secure even if everything about the system, except the key, is public knowledge. Cryptographers know this as **Kerckhoffs' law**.

Kerckhoffs' book also contained important advances in cryptanalysis. The eminent historian of cryptology, David Kahn, argues that Kerckhoff's book established that 'ordeal by cryptanalysis is the only sure trial for military cryptography' – a principle that still holds true today.

Its publication certainly had a major impact on cryptology in his own time, too. The government bought hundreds of copies, it became widely read and stimulated a cryptographic revival throughout France. And in the build-up to the First World War, that French advantage in cryptology would prove to be invaluable.

THE DORABELLA CIPHER –
ELGAR'S OTHER ENIGMA

Above: Edward Elgar (1857–1934).

Edward Elgar, one of Britain's most famous com-
posers, was fascinated by codes and riddles. His
well-loved composition 'Variations on an original
theme', for example, is generally known as the
'Enigma' variations because of a cryptic com-

ment in the programme notes for its first-ever
performance, in 1899.

'The Enigma I will not explain,' he wrote. 'Its
"dark saying" must be left unguessed, and I warn
you that the apparent connexion between the
Variations and the Theme is often of the slightest
texture; further, through and over the whole set
another and larger theme "goes", but is not played.'

But Elgar's fascination with hidden meanings
extended beyond the musical realm. This is
perhaps unsurprising, as there are several
similarities between the work of a composer and
that of a codebreaker – both have to shuffle and
transpose parallel sequences of code or notes
to find the best fit. His letters to friends were
filled with word play and musical riddles, and
one of the Elgar family homes was named 'Craeg
Lea', an anagram of (C)arice, (A)lice and
(E)dward ELGAR.

One of the most famous examples of Elgar's
love of cryptography dates from some two years
before the premiere of the Enigma variations. On
14 July 1897, Elgar sent a letter to a young friend
written in a cipher that to this day has evaded a
satisfactory solution. The message consists of
87 characters and appears to use a 24-letter
alphabet in which each symbol consists of one,
two or three semi-circles, orientated in one of
eight directions. Frequency analysis (see pages
24–25) suggests that Elgar used a simple
substitution cipher based on a plaintext in
English, a theory that is backed up by the
number of characters used in the alphabet – in
many ciphers, I and J share a single character, as

Above: The Dorabella cipher Below: Dora Penny

do U and V – but no-one has yet been able to decipher the message along these lines. Some cryptanalysts have used a key found in one of Elgar's exercise books, in which he listed the symbols used in the Dorabella cipher and matched them to the letters of the alphabet. However, when this key is applied to the Dorabella cipher, it does not generate anything that makes obvious sense. This seems to suggest that Elgar used a more complex method of encryption, perhaps using a keyword to encipher the message still further.

The recipient of the letter was Dora Penny, the 22-year-old daughter of Alfred Penny, Rector of St Peter's, Wolverhampton. From the late 1890s until 1913, Penny had formed a close relationship with Elgar and his wife, Alice, as she recounted in her book *Edward Elgar: Memories of a Variation*. At the time the encrypted letter was sent, Dora and the Elgars had met on several occasions. 'It is well known,' wrote Dora, 'that Elgar was always interested in puzzles, ciphers,

cryptograms and the like. The cipher here reproduced – the third letter I had from him, if indeed it is one – came to me enclosed in a letter from [Elgar's wife] to my stepmother. On the back of it is written 'Miss Penny'. It followed upon their visit to us at Wolverhampton in July 1897.

I have never had the slightest idea what message it conveys; he never explained it and all attempts to solve it have failed. Should any reader of this book succeed in arriving at a solution it would interest me very much to hear of it.'

Dora was herself the inspiration for the tenth variation (Dorabella) in the Enigma variations, so some have speculated that the cipher Elgar sent her might offer a clue as to the deeper mystery of the composition. When, in later life, she asked him about the secret of the Enigma, he replied, 'I thought you, of all people, would guess it'. Dora died in 1964, so if she alone held the secret to these puzzles, it may be that the hope of a solution died with her.

CHAPTER FOUR

Perseverance

Sheer bloody-mindedness helped crack Enigma and other wartime ciphers. The Zimmerman telegram, the ADFGX cipher, Cold War codes, Venona codes and the Navajo Code talkers.

The flow of history, particularly in wartime, can hinge on the success or failure to break ciphers. Unbroken, a cipher can be one of the most potent weapons in any nation's arsenal. Military chiefs can send messages to their front-line troops, safe in the knowledge that their strategies are not being anticipated by the opposing forces. Broken, a cipher can be turned against its master. If your enemy can read your most secret messages, yet you remain unaware that your encryption has been compromised, they can ruin your best-laid military plans.

This means that in most recent wars, cryptologists and cryptanalysts have faced each other in a very real combat, with the fortunes of war depending very much on which of them has the upper hand. Codemakers and breakers have thus been on the front line, if not physically, then mentally. And unlike many of those who engage in the physical elements of combat, their efforts often remain clouded in secrecy, only to be revealed years or decades later when the codes that they have crafted and destroyed have become irrelevant – except to history.

Opposite: 1914, British soldiers in the trenches during World War I, trying to break the German lines from Epehy to Bellicourt.

WORLD WAR I – THE ZIMMERMAN TELEGRAM

The Zimmerman telegram is a classic example of the use of coded messages in wartime, and it can be argued that it is the single most important example of successful cryptanalysis and the subsequent deciphering changing the course of war.

The telegram was sent on 16 January 1917 by the German Foreign Secretary, Arthur Zimmerman, to the German ambassador to Mexico, Heinrich von Eckardt. Unbeknown to the Germans, the content of the message was intercepted by the British codebreaking team Room 40, named after their location in the Admiralty building in London's Whitehall. The team was formed just after the start of the First World War and remained at the heart of British codebreaking efforts until it was superseded by the Government Code and Cypher School in 1919, a merger of the cryptology units of the Admiralty and the War Office.

The telegram's message, encrypted using a code known as 0075, was deciphered in part using captured German code-books that related to a previous version of the cipher.

Below: Royal Air Force recruits learning Morse code at a training station in 1945.

The translation of the deciphered telegram read as follows:

'We intend to begin on the first of February unrestricted submarine warfare. We shall endeavour in spite of this to keep the United States of America neutral. In the event of this not succeeding, we make Mexico a proposal of alliance on the following basis: make war together, make peace together, generous financial support, and an understanding on our part that Mexico is to reconquer the lost territory in Texas, New Mexico, and Arizona. The settlement in detail is left to you. You will inform the President of the above most secretly as soon as the outbreak of war with the United States of America is certain and add the suggestion that he should, on his own initiative, invite Japan to immediate adherence and at the same time mediate between Japan and ourselves. Please call the President's attention to the fact that the ruthless employment of our submarines now offers the prospect of compelling England in a few months to make peace.'

Zimmerman

Above: The original Zimmerman Telegram.

But having deciphered the Zimmerman telegram, British intelligence faced a dilemma faced by many cryptanalysts. They knew that the telegram was political dynamite – revealing its contents would force the United States into declaring war on Germany, but at the same time would indicate to the Germans that their cipher had been broken.

Then the problem was taken from their hands. A British agent in Mexico uncovered another copy of the telegram in a public telegraph office, which had been encrypted using an earlier German cipher. The telegram's contents were passed on to the US government and the message was published in American newspapers on 1 March 1917. The US Congress declared war on Germany and its Allies just over a month later.

It can therefore be argued that the deciphering of the Zimmerman telegram and the subsequent US entry into the First World War hastened the end of the war and changed the course of history.

WORLD WAR I – THE ADFGX CIPHER

Some advances in cryptology are made by combining previous encryption techniques. The ADFGX and ADFGVX ciphers used by Germany in the First World War combined Polybius squares (as discussed in Chapter 1) and transposition, and were invented by Colonel Fritz Nebel. The ADFGX cipher was first used in March 1918.

To make matters even more difficult for codebreakers, both the Polybius square and transposition key were changed on a daily basis. Codebreakers in Britain's Room 40 and the French Bureau du Chiffre worked constantly to find a chink in the encryption scheme.

CODE ANALYSIS

A Polybius square is formed using the letters A, D, F, G and X instead of the numbers 1 to 5 and the letters of the alphabet randomly scattered throughout the square. This seemingly odd choice of letters was made because of the relative difficulty of confusing those characters when they were sent in Morse code – essential if you want to minimise the risk of the message being garbled. Since there are only 25 spaces in the square and 26 letters of the alphabet, the letters i and j are used interchangeably.

Table 1

	A	D	F	G	X
A	f	n	w	c	l
D	y	r	h	i/j	v
F	t	a	o	u	d
G	s	g	b	m	z
X	e	x	k	p	q

Now, imagine we want to encrypt the following message: 'See you in Leningrad'. The first letter of the message is **s** and this appears in the square at the point where there is a **G** in the left-hand column and **A** in the top row. Thus the letter **s** is encrypted as **GA**. Similarly, the next letter, **e**, is encrypted as **XA**.

The whole message is thus encrypted as follows (spaces are ignored):

Table 2

S	e	e	y	o	u	i	n	L	e	n	i	n	g	r	a	d
GA	XA	XA	DA	FF	FG	DG	AD	AX	XA	AD	DG	AD	GD	DD	FD	FX

To make decryption more difficult, a transposition cipher is now used on the encrypted characters in the second row. A key word is chosen, *Kaiser*, for example. The transposition is carried out in columns as shown below, with spaces left where the message does not fill the grid:

Table 3

K	A	I	S	E	R
G	A	X	A	X	A
D	A	F	F	F	G
D	G	A	D	A	X
X	A	A	D	D	G
A	D	G	D	D	D
F	D	F	X		

The columns are then reorganised into alphabetical order according to the letters in the keyword, as seen below:

Table 4

A	E	I	K	R	S
A	X	X	G	A	A
A	F	F	D	G	F
G	A	A	D	X	D
A	D	A	X	G	D
D	D	G	A	D	D
D		F	F		X

These columns are then written out reading downwards to give the ciphertext:

AAGADD XFADD XFAAGF GDDXAF AFDDDX

This is the encrypted message, which during the First World War would have been transmitted in Morse code. Note that the blocks of letters vary in length – some have six characters, others have five. These variable length blocks make the message incredibly difficult to crack.

Above: Georges-Jean Panvin (1886–1980).

CRACKING ADFGX: FROM MINING TO CODEBREAKING

Georges-Jean Painvin, born in Nantes in 1886, was an unlikely codebreaker. He studied at a mining college, then became a lecturer at colleges in St Etienne and Paris, specialising in palaeontology.

However, in the early years of the First World War he became friends with Captain Paulier, a cryptologist in the French Sixth Army, and soon became interested in the code work Paulier was doing. Following inspired work on an earlier cipher, Painvin was invited to work in secret with the Bureau du Chiffre on cracking German codes.

The first use of the ADFGX cipher by the Germans came just as they launched their last major offensive of the war. In late March 1918, German forces launched an attack near Arras in northern France. The intention was to divide the French and British forces and to take the strategically important area surrounding Amiens. For the Allies, breaking the cipher suddenly became critically important.

One of the most obvious things about the encrypted German messages was that they contained just five letters repeated. This led Painvin and other Allied cryptanalysts to believe they were working with some form of square cipher. Frequency analysis soon showed that the encryption was not a simple Polybius square.

The huge increase in the number of messages following the March offensive gave Painvin a second breakthrough. He spotted patterns in the encrypted messages, suggesting that the same words were appearing at the beginning of several messages. Since the messages in any one day were encrypted using the same two keys, he believed that these repetitions could be a crib – a sample of encrypted text whose true meaning is known or can be guessed, for example, salutations, titles or weather conditions.

Painvin finally managed to break the ADFGX cipher on 5 April. In fact, the thing that made the cipher seem difficult to crack – the variable length of the blocks – came to Painvin's aid. If you refer to table 3, you will notice that the columns containing six encrypted characters are all at the left-hand side of the grid, while those at the right all contain five.

Table 3

K	A	I	S	E	R
G	A	X	A	X	A
D	A	F	F	F	G
D	G	A	D	A	X
X	A	A	D	D	G
A	D	G	D	D	D
F	D	F	X		

This dramatically cut down the number of column orderings Painvin had to try. He then used frequency analysis to see which column order gave letter frequencies that corresponded with what you might expect for a typical German block of text. This was no trivial matter. Painvin used 18 messages to help decrypt the cipher, and it took him four days and nights of uninterrupted work. Even when he knew the encryption scheme, deciphering the messages still took time.

A potentially serious problem emerged on 1 June when the intercepted messages received following a new German offensive at Aisne started to include an additional letter – V. However, Painvin took just a single day to work out that this new ADFGVX cipher simply used a six by six square for the initial encryption, using all 26 letters of the alphabet and the digits zero to nine.

The difficulties Painvin faced are perhaps best highlighted by the fact that only ten ADFGX and ADFGVX cipher keys in total were discovered by the end of the war. Afterwards, Painvin returned to the mining industry and followed a successful industrial career. As with many of the heroes of cryptanalysis, his efforts were not made public until much later. He was made an officer of France's Legion of Honour in 1933 and made a Grand Officer in 1973, seven years before his death.

WORLD WAR II – ENIGMA AND BLETCHLEY PARK

The story of Enigma and its role in the Second World War has become one of the most widely known in codebreaking, despite the fact that the full story only became known decades after the end of the war.

Between the First and Second World Wars, Britain's codebreakers working for the Government Code and Cypher School (GC&CS), the successor to Room 40, practised by deciphering diplomatic and commercial messages from many nations, the Soviet Union, Spain, and the United States in particular. As war approached, the focus of the school's efforts moved to Germany, Italy and Japan, and more people were employed by the service. Bletchley Park, or BP as it was more often known to its wartime inhabitants, is a small mansion about 50 miles north-west of London. It was purchased in 1938 by the head of the British intelligence service MI6 as a home for the rapidly growing GC&CS, and given the cover name 'Station X'.

As the Second World War approached, 186 people worked at BP, 50 of whom were focused on encryption rather than decryption.

As war raged across Europe, the number of messages being sent by the Germans and their allies multiplied rapidly. This situation was further compounded by the fact that each military service used a different version of the Enigma machine to encipher their messages, creating a vast amount of work for the BP staff.

On the orders of British Prime Minister Winston Churchill, the number of codebreakers working at BP on cracking the messages increased. These men and women were typically mathematicians and linguists, many of them from the universities of Oxford and Cambridge – BP is almost equidistant between the two cities, and was therefore perfectly situated. In 1943, American codebreakers joined their British counterparts as the United States entered into the war. By May 1945, there were almost 9,000 staff, plus a further 2,500 working on related issues elsewhere.

Below: Codebreakers at work in the machine room of hut 6, Bletchley Park, 1943.

Right: Operating the Enigma machine at Bletchley Park during the Second World War.

This rapid increase in staffing meant that more working space had to be built at BP and a proliferation of huts and other buildings appeared, known simply by a number or letter, and each with a different function. Hut 8, for example, housed the cryptanalysts working on Germany's Naval Enigma ciphers. Hut 6 focused on breaking the German Army and Air Force Enigma ciphers. In E Block, the decrypted and translated messages from Enigma were re-encrypted and transmitted to Allied military chiefs.

HOW THE POLISH CRACKED ENIGMA

The Polish contribution to the cracking of Enigma was fundamental and began as early as 1932. A trio of young Polish cryptologists were at the forefront of the work – the mathematicians Marian Rejewski, Jerzy Rozycki and Henryk Zygalski.

Initially, messages sent with Enigma included the individual rotor settings encrypted twice in succession at the beginning. The user's manual for the machines might say that on the fourth of the month, the rotors should be set with the letters A, X and N uppermost. The operator would then begin the message with the six characters AXNAXN, before continuing with the body of the message.

The Poles discovered they could use features of a branch of pure mathematics known as group theory in order to break the cipher. What they realised was that for any given configuration of the Enigma machine, any letter entered would be enciphered as another letter. Because the machine was reversible, that enciphered letter would then be enciphered as the original letter used. It was this realisation that gave the Poles a way into Enigma.

We can write out the way one setting of an Enigma machine transposes characters using group theory notation:

A B C D E F G H I J K L M N O P Q R S T U V W X Y Z
J R U X A W N S F Q Y T B H M D E V G I L P K Z C O

What this shorthand notation means is that when the letters in the top row are typed into an Enigma machine, they light up the lamp showing the letter in the bottom row. For example, when you press **A** it lights up the **J** lamp and when you press **T**, the **I** lamp is lit. This can then be reduced into letter cycles.

Notice how **A** transposes as **J**, **J** transposes as **Q**, **Q** transposes to **E** and **E** back to **A**, the letter we started with. This can be written as (**A J Q E**).

There are also three other cycles:

(G N H S)
(B R V P D X Z O M)
(C U L T I F W K Y)

The Poles realised that these cycles always occurred in pairs of equal length; in this case, two pairs of cycles with four letters and two with nine letters. This realisation reduced the amount of manual effort required to break the cipher. They also found that the steckering of letter pairs (see page 103) had no impact on the underlying group theory. If pairs of letters were interchanged by steckering, the number and length of these cycles remained exactly the same. A paper by Rejewski at the time mentioned they were able to obtain these stecker settings, but went into no detail about how this was achieved.

THE ENIGMA MACHINE

Dr Arthur Scherbius, an engineer living in Berlin, developed the first Enigma machine in the 1920s as a means of encrypting commercial messages. The German government adopted the machine three years later, making substantial modifications to improve the security that the device offered.

The Enigma machine was a portable encryption machine about the same size as the processor unit of a desktop computer. A keyboard at the front of the machine was used to type in the message. Above the keyboard was a series of 26 lamps, each showing a letter of the alphabet. When a key was pressed, one of the lamps lit up, showing what that letter needed to be replaced with in the encrypted text. The letters were then noted down by a second operator, who then sent the encrypted message using Morse code. These messages were then picked up by the intended recipients, who typed them into their own Enigma machine, set up in the same way as the sender's, and obtained the original message. However, eavesdroppers could also pick up these encrypted radio messages, and that is exactly what the Allies did through a series of radio listening posts. Even if eavesdroppers had their own Enigma machine, it would need to be set up in the same way as the sender's to decode the message. The internal complexity of the Enigma machine made this incredibly difficult.

Inside the original version of the machine were three rotating cylinders, or rotors. Each rotor had a series of internal wirings and electrical contacts on their faces so that every different position of the rotor resulted in a different electrical connection between the keyboard keys and the lamps. When a key was pressed, the rightmost rotor rotated by one character in a similar way to a milometer in a car. After 26 rotations, the middle rotor would then rotate by one character. After 26 rotations of this rotor, the leftmost rotor would rotate. These turn-overs, as they were called, were effected by a notch in the rotor ring. However, to increase the complexity of the encryption, it was possible for the operator to set the notch on each ring to 26 different positions.

Opposite: An Enigma machine. Above: Rotor from an Enigma machine. The green wires on the right made an electrical connection between the keyboard and the display, where the encrypted version of each letter would light up.

This might mean that the middle rotor might rotate after the first 10 characters had been typed and only then after every 26th rotation.

A reflector at the end of the rotors meant that the signal went back through the three rotors by a different route than on the way through.

Although these elements gave an almost unimaginable number of possible settings, the complexity of the encryption was further increased by a plugboard at the front of the machine. With this, specific pairs of letters could be interchanged by inserting cables between the plugs (or steckers as they subsequently became known to codebreakers, using the original German word) marked with those letters.

According to Frank Carter and John Gallehawk, there were 158 million million million possible different ways of setting up the machine at the beginning of the cipher process. It is little wonder that the Germans had high confidence in its ability to keep messages secret.

Although it is often imagined that British and American codebreakers did not have access to an Enigma machine until just before the start of the war, in fact they had one of Scherbius' commercial machines as early as 1926, purchased in Vienna by Dilly Knox, a member of CC&CS. Indeed, it has subsequently been revealed that the patents for the commercial Enigma machine had been lodged with the British patent office in the 1920s.

However, complex mathematics on its own was not enough. To use these theories, they needed to construct a card-based catalogue listing all the possible permutations for the more than 100,000 possible rotor configurations, a hugely arduous task without the benefit of a computer.

The Polish codebreakers also built a machine known as the cyclometer, constructed from two Enigma rotors, and used it to generate these permutations more quickly.

The cyclometer was used to prepare a catalogue of the length and number of cycles in the 'characteristics' for all 17,576 positions of the rotors for a given sequence of rotors. Since there were six such possible sequences, the resulting 'catalogue of characteristics', or 'card catalogue', comprised a total of 6 x 17,576 = 105,456 entries.

Rejewski wrote that the preparation of the catalog, 'was laborious and took over a year, but when it was ready ... daily keys [could be obtained] within about fifteen minutes'.

ENCRYPTING THE ENCRYPTION

In 1938, the Germans changed the way Enigma machines were operated. Instead of using the common rotor starting positions in the manual, every operator chose his own settings. The start settings were transmitted unencrypted. So, for example, the message might start with AXN as before. However, the operator would then think of a different rotor start setting that would be used to encrypt the message itself, HVO, say. He would then type this into the Enigma machine twice – HVOHVO. However, because the machine had already been set up with the initial AXN setting, it would encrypt HVOHVO as something entirely different – EYMEHY, for example. It is important to notice that there is no repetition in this encrypted version, since with each character typed the rotors move on by one position. Thus, the message sent by the operator would begin AXNEYMEHY and be followed by the message encrypted using HVO rotor settings.

On receiving this message, the recipient would see instantly that he should set his rotors to AXN initially. Typing in EYMEHY would then give him HVOHVO, and he would reset the rotors to the HVO position. The rest of the message would then be unencrypted as he typed.

This new complication invalidated the catalogue method developed by the Poles and must have been a soul-destroying experience after so much time and resources were invested in it. However, they soon discovered another method, again using mathematical group theory.

You will notice in our example of the rotor settings above that the message settings were encrypted as EYMEHY and that the first and fourth characters are the same – the letter E. Rejewski and his colleagues noticed that this repetition of individual characters in the first and fourth positions (and also the second and fith and the third and sixth) happened relatively frequently. The instances where this occurred came to be known as 'females'.

The Poles built six machines called 'bombas', each of which comprised three Enigma rotors mechanically coupled together, which mechanically searched for rotor settings that would produce such females. Six were produced so that all possible orders of rotor could be checked at the same time – i.e. AXN, ANX, NAX, NXA, XAN and XNA.

However, using the bombas in this way relied on none of the letters involved being steckered. Initially, just three letter pairs were steckered, but later the Germans increased this to ten pairs, so Zygalski devised an alternative method using perforated sheets of cardboard.

The process of creating these 'Zygalski sheets' was very time consuming, as large numbers of sheets were required and the perforations – often up to a thousand per sheet – were made by hand using razor blades.

26 sheets were created, each one representing one possible starting position of the left-hand rotor in the Enigma machine. On each sheet, a 26 x 26 grid was marked with the letters A to Z down the left-hand side and A to Z across the top. The letters on the left represented the starting position of the middle rotor while those across the top represented the initial starting position of the right-hand rotor.

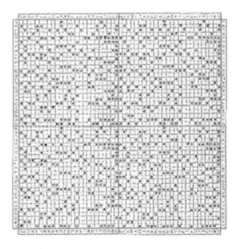

Below: Example of a Zygalski sheet.

We know that our message starting AXN EYMEHY contains a female where the first and fourth characters of the message settings are the same. This means that on the Zygalski sheet representing the letter A in the left-hand rotor position, there would be a hole perforated on the grid at the point where X on the left-hand column meets N from the top row.

If other messages are transmitted on the same day by the same operator, and also include females in their message settings, we can start to stack sheets together so that their grids overlap exactly. When this stack of sheets is held up to the light, only those settings where there the holes overlap – and the light shines through – are possible settings that day. Each sheet added to the pile reduced the number of potential start settings still further. Given enough messages of the right format, the initial message settings might ultimately be deduced.

In December 1938, even this method became impractical, when the Germans introduced a new sophistication to the system. Instead of using three rotors in any permutation, operators could now choose any three rotors from a set of five. This increased the number of rotor settings tenfold and the task of creating the necessary sheets was beyond the codebreakers' resources.

Events soon overtook the Poles. With the impending invasion of the country, they realised they needed to share their work with others. As Germany prepared to invade, the Poles gave locally-built replicas of military Enigma machines to both GC&CS and French intelligence.

Below: Alan Turing (1912–1954), who devised a number of techniques for breaking German ciphers, including the 'bombe', which could find settings for the Enigma machine.

BREAKING ENIGMA

In order to decrypt a message, the recipient – and any eavesdropper – needed to know which three rotors had been chosen and their positions in the machine, where the turn-over

notches had been set, which starting positions had been used for each rotor (as indicated by the letters shown in the small windows at the top right) and which letters had been interchanged using the steckers.

It was the increased number of stecker pairs that gave Bletchley Park's codebreakers their biggest challenge. For each rotor setting, there were more than 2.5 million million million possible plugboard settings. This seemingly impossible task was made easier with the invention of an electrical device known as a 'bombe', conceived by the Cambridge mathematicians Alan Turing and Gordon Welchman. The name reflected the Polish 'bomba', but was in fact a totally different device.

Essential to this approach was being able to find what is known as a crib. If you consider the nature of written correspondence, it is highly structured. For example, when you write a letter to someone, you often begin with 'Dear Sir/Madam' and end with 'Yours faithfully'.

This was also the case with many of Germany's wartime messages, although the structured elements were often different. Messages might

Above: The 'bombe'.

frequently begin with the word 'secret', while messages from naval vessels often included the weather and their position. One operator was particularly fond of using IST – the German word for is – as his message setting. Another operator in Bari frequently used the initials of his girlfriend as the starting positions of the rotors. Breaking Enigma, then, was as much about highlighting human frailties as technical ones.

Finding the correct position of this crib in the ciphertext was not child's play – some Enigma operators prefixed often-repeated phrases or words with dummy characters to confound potential codebreakers.

The design of the bombe allowed its operators to check the 26 possible stecker partners of a given input letter simultaneously for each of the nearly 18,000 possible rotor settings. As it ran through these settings, if it came across a series of settings that corresponded with the crib, it stopped. Manual techniques, such as frequency analysis, were then used to test these rotor settings. If the frequency of letters corresponded generally with what would be expected from a typical German text, then other stecker pairs would be suggested. Eventually, from all this hard work and a huge amount of good fortune, they would arrive at the original message settings used for that day's messages, though this did not happen every day.

One interesting technique used by BP was known as 'gardening'. This involved provoking the German forces to include known words in their messages. For example, if an area had been cleared of mines, BP's codebreakers would request of the Army that the area be mined again in the hope that the Germans would include the word *minen* in messages emanating from the area.

The first Enigma message was broken at Bletchley Park on 20 January 1940, but it was of vital importance not to let Germany know that the Allies were now able to read many of its messages. In order to hide the existence and success of Bletchley Park, the British

Government invented a spy with the codename Boniface, and an imaginary network of agents in the Fatherland. Thus, messages would be sent to various parts of the British military that implied that Boniface, or one of his spies in Germany, had overheard a conversation between high-ranking German officers, or had found a classified document in a wastebin. This way, if the information was leaked back to the Germans, they would not realise that their wireless signals were being eavesdropped.

By the end of the war, the Bletchley Park team had broken more than two and a half million Enigma messages, and had made highly significant contributions to the Allied victory. Certainly, the D-Day landings would have been considerably more difficult without the ability to decode German messages. The ability of Bletchley Park's codebreakers to read Enigma code in all probability shortened the war.

Above: Reinforcements disembarking at a Normandy beach during the Allied invasion of France on D-Day (6 June 1944).

INVISIBLE INK AND OTHER TOOLS OF THE SPYING TRADE

About 10 minutes past midnight on 13 June 1942, four men from a German U-boat came ashore on Long Island, New York with the aim of sabotaging the production of American equipment and supplies and striking fear into the US population.

The men had come laden with $175,200 in US currency and enough explosives to fuel a two-year campaign, but within 48 hours, their mission faltered. On the evening of 14 June, the leader of the group, George John Dasch, lost his nerve and turned himself in with a call to the FBI in New York.

Within days, he had been taken into custody and thoroughly interrogated. FBI agents going through Dasch's things came across a handkerchief that they subjected to a test using ammonia fumes. The test revealed invisible writing in a copper sulphate compound, listing incriminating names, addresses and contacts for Dasch's group and another party of saboteurs who had come ashore in Florida. The plot was revealed, and Dasch and another spy by the name of Ernest Burger were the only two of the eight men not put to death the following month.

Like the Nazi saboteurs, spies throughout history have used invisible ink and other forms of steganography to hide information from their enemies. Working incognito, it isn't enough for a spy to disguise the meaning of a message with cryptography – he or she needs to hide the fact that there is a message there at all.

One technique makes use of a pack of cards. The pack is arranged into an agreed order, and a message written on the side of the deck. Once the pack is shuffled, the marks on the side of the pack become almost invisible until the desired recipient rearranges them.

In ancient Greece, Aeneas the Tactician also described a technique that involved poking tiny holes in a book or message above or below existing letters as a way of conveying secret words – very similar methods were still in use during twentieth-century wars.

Another means of hiding large amounts of secret information in a tiny space was reportedly developed by the Germans during World War II.

Opposite: German spy Ernest Burger, arrested after one of the men turned himself in to the FBI.
Above: German submarines off the US coast in 1942.

This trick, called a microdot, consists of an image – for example of a secret document – that has been photographed and reduced to the size of a type-written full-stop. The miniscule size of the dots allowed them to be concealed in letters or telegrams sent through the normal channels. The intended recipient could then read the dot's contents with a microscope.

In modern times, steganography has entered the digital realm. Digital pictures or audio files, which contain large amounts of data, have been used to hide messages. By making subtle changes to the binary code for the file, it is possible to embed data that could go unnoticed.

HOW TO MAKE INVISIBLE INK

Invisible ink can be made from a wide variety of substances, some of which you probably have around the house. The simplest are citrus juices, onion juice or milk. By dipping a brush, pen nib or even your finger into the juice and writing on a piece of paper, you can inscribe an invisible message. These inks will be made visible with the heat of a light bulb or iron. In the case of lemon juice, this is because the paper that has absorbed some of the acidic juice browns at a lower temperature than the rest of the paper.

Another easily obtained invisible ink is vinegar, which is revealed by red cabbage water. A host of other chemicals can be used, including copper and iron sulphates and ammonia.

When writing in invisible ink, it's a good idea to write a decoy message on the paper using a normal ball-point pen, since blank paper might look suspicious.

HITLER'S CIPHER

Variations on Enigma were used for most of the secret messages the German military were exchanging. However, some messages – principally those sent by Hitler to his various generals – were considered too secret for even that supposedly secure means of encryption.

Messages that had been encrypted using a cipher system other than Enigma were first intercepted in 1940. The codebreakers at BP gave messages encrypted in this way the generic nickname 'Fish'.

It later emerged that a machine much larger than the portable Enigma machines was used to encrypt these messages. The Lorenz SZ40 used 12 rotors, and as a result was almost unimaginably more complex than Enigma. Of course, the only way that the codebreakers at BP were aware of the machine was through the encrypted messages it produced. They gave this unseen machine the nickname 'Tunny', after the fish of the same name. Later in the war, other encryption machines used by the Germans were also given fishy nicknames: 'Sturgeon', for example.

CODE ANALYSIS

The SZ in the Lorenz machine name stood for *Schlüsselzusatz*, or additive key, and this gives the basis on which the machine encrypted its text. The machine represented letters using a five-character-long string of binary zeros and ones. For example, the letter A was 11000, while L was 01001.

Each letter was encrypted by combining its binary representation with the representation of another letter using an operation known as exclusive-or (XOR). This operation has the following properties on individual binary digits:

---

0 XOR 0 = 0
0 XOR 1 = 1
1 XOR 0 = 1
1 XOR 1 = 0

So, if the letters A and L were combined, it would produce the following:

A =	1 1 0 0 0
L =	0 1 0 0 1
XOR	1 0 0 0 1

Now 10001 is the representation for the letter Z, so the Lorenz machine would encipher A as Z in this case.

The recipient of the message would do the same in reverse.

	Z = 1 0 0 0 1
	L = 0 1 0 0 1
XOR	1 1 0 0 0

This returns the binary representation of the letter A we first started with.

The key to the Lorenz machine's complexity was the seeming randomness of the added letter, generated by those 12 rotors. Like in Enigma, the Lorenz machine's rotors rotated after each letter. Five of them rotated in a regular manner, while five rotated according to the settings of two pin wheels. Breaking the Fish messages thus relied on finding the correct initial rotor settings.

However, BP's codebreakers managed to work out how Tunny was constructed thanks to a mistake on the part of a German cipher operator in August 1941. A long message was sent by the operator, but it was corrupted in transmission. The operator resent the message using the same key, but with a few of the words abbreviated. Both messages were intercepted by Allied listening stations and relayed to BP. This enabled Allied cryptanalysts to work out the basic design and build an emulator, *Heath Robinson*, named after the cartoonist famous for drawing crackpot inventions. Unfortunately, this emulator proved too slow and unreliable, taking several days to break the messages involved.

Part of the problem was keeping two punched paper tapes travelling at high speed in synchronisation. BP's Alan Turing had previously worked with a young telephone engineer called Tommy Flowers when constructing the bombes used for decoding Enigma, and asked for his help again. Flowers suggested building a machine that replaced one of the paper tapes with a series of valves that acted like digital switches, eliminating the synchronisation problems.

It took ten months and 1,500 valves to build the machine, and the first was installed and began work at BP in December 1943. The machine, *Colossus*, was the world's first programmable computer. It was the size of a room and weighed a tonne, but the valve technology meant that *Colossus* could crack a Lorenz-encrypted message in hours rather than days. It worked by comparing the two data streams, counting each match based on a programmable function. An improved *Coloussus Mark II* was installed in June 1944, and by the end of the war, 10 *Colossi* with an even higher number of valves were in use at BP.

Above and opposite: The *Colossus* machine, the world's first programmable computer.

PURPLE AND PEARL HARBOR

During the Second World War, Japan was also encoding its messages. For its high-level diplomatic messages, the Japanese had started using in 1938 a machine known as the 97-shiki oobun Inji-ki, which took input in the form of Latin characters – the same as the English alphabet – and not Japanese katakana characters. The cipher produced by this machine became known to the American codebreakers as 'Purple', following a tradition for naming the Japanese ciphers after colours.

Unlike the Enigma machine, the Purple machine did not use rotors, but stepping switches similar to those found in telephone exchanges. Each switch had 25 positions, and stepped to the next position when an electric pulse was applied.

Inside the machine, the alphabet was divided into two groups, one of six letters (the vowels plus the letter Y) and one of 20 (the consonants). For the vowels, there was a switch that stepped once for each character input. However, there were three connected 25-position switches for the consonants, rotating like the odometer on a car.

Like the Germans and Enigma, the Japanese believed that the Purple cipher was unbreakable. However, a team at the US Army Signals Intelligence Service (SIS), led by the service's chief William F. Friedman and cryptanalyst Frank Rowlett, managed to crack it.

Perhaps the biggest advance in breaking Purple was made by SIS's Leo Rosen, who managed to build a replica of the Japanese machine. Astonishingly, when a fragment of one of the machines was found at the Japanese Embassy in Berlin at the end of the war, it turned out that Rosen had used exactly the same stepping switch in his replica – an inspired guess indeed.

With this replica, and a cryptanalytical approach to discovering the keys used by the machine, SIS was decrypting large numbers of Purple-encrypted messages by the end of 1940. The cryptanalytical techniques used in breaking Purple were similar to those used in breaking the

Opposite: Japan's Purple machine.　Above: The Japanese attack on Pearl Harbor, 7 December 1941.

Enigma cipher. Frequently used salutations and closing remarks were used as cribs, while messages that had been transmitted more than once in error were used to crack this 'uncrackable' cipher.

Cracking the basis of Purple did not mean that every message was instantly readable – there were still the message keys to uncover, so intelligence flowing from SIS's breakthrough was at best patchy. There was also the problem of distributing the intelligence gained from reading encrypted messages. Because of the necessary secrecy involved, many who received the intelligence did not recognise its value.

Before America's entry into the Second World War, the United States and Japan were locked in a largely economic battle over dominance of the Pacific. Some of the decrypted messages would

have given the US Government an insight into how Japan was saying one thing through diplomatic channels, but actually doing another surreptitiously. However, many codebreaking experts believe that being able to read some Purple messages led to a US complacency that was to be brutally shattered just a few years later.

On 7 December 1941, a Purple-encrypted message intercepted from the Japanese Embassy breaking off diplomatic relations with the US was decrypted, but the message did not reach the US State Department in enough time to realise that it related to the subsequent attack on Pearl Harbor. However, there was no specific reference to the attack in the message, so it seems unlikely that anything could have been done in time in any case.

NAVAJO CODE TALKERS

The brutal conflict waged by US and Japanese forces across the Pacific arena during the Second World War was also a high-stakes cryptographic battle.

For their part, the Japanese army had groomed a team of well-trained English-speaking soldiers who could be put to use intercepting communications and sabotaging the message. The American military had its own sophisticated cryptographic systems at its disposal, such as the SIGABA cipher machine, developed by SIS's Frank Rowlett.

Below: Navajo Marines operating a portable radio set behind the Bougainville front lines, Solomon Islands, in December 1943.

This machine, also known as the Electric Code Machine Mark II, avoided the single-step rotor or switch motion found in the Enigma and Purple machines, since this made cracking the resulting ciphertext easier. SIGABA employed a punched paper tape that effectively randomised how much each rotor advanced after each letter was typed, making it much more difficult for eavesdroppers to decipher. It is generally believed that no-one managed to decipher SIGABA's messages while it was in general use.

The disadvantage of SIGABA was that it was expensive, very large and complex, and was of little use in the field. In combat, delays could hurt. During fighting on the island of Guadalcanal, for example, military chiefs complained that it often took more than two hours to send and decode messages because of the fragility of the machine and its slowness in encrypting. The US forces wanted a faster system – and in early 1942, First World War veteran Philip Johnston, an engineer living in California, came up with the perfect solution.

Johnston was the son of a missionary and had lived among the Navajo people from the age of four, an upbringing that meant he was one of the very few non-Navajos who could speak their language fluently. In 1942, after reading a newspaper article about Native Americans who served in the Second World War, he had the idea that the notoriously impenetrable language could be used to send secure messages quickly – from one Navajo signalman to another.

Within days, Johnston had presented his idea to Major J.E. Jones, force communication officer at Camp Elliot. On 28 February, a demonstration for officers showed that two Navajo men could encode, transmit and decode a three-line message in twenty seconds – something the code machines of the day needed 30 minutes to achieve.

The Navajo trainees helped to compile the lexicon, and they tended to choose words describing the natural world to indicate specific military terms. Thus, the names of birds replaced types of planes, and fish replaced ships.

Soon enough, 29 Navajo men had been recruited for the mission and set to work creating the first Navajo code.

NAVAJO CODE

Actual word	Code word	Navajo Translation
Fighter Plane	Hummingbird	Da-he-tih-hi
Observation Plane	Owl	Ne-as-jah Torpedo
Plane	Swallow	Tas-chizzie
Bomber	Buzzards	Jay-sho
Dive Bomber	Chicken Hawk	Gini
Bombs	Eggs	A-ye-shi
Amphibious Vehicle	Frog	Chal
Battleship	Whale	Lo-tso
Destroyer	Shark	Ca-lo
Submarine	Iron fish	Besh-lo

The complete lexicon contained 274 words, but there were still problems in translating unpredictable words, or the names of people and places. The solution was to devise an encoded alphabet for spelling out difficult words. For example, the word Navy could be translated into Navajo as 'nesh-chee (nut) wol-la-chee (ant) a-keh-di-glin (victor) tsah-as-zoh (yucca)'. There were also several variations for each letter. The Navajo words 'wol-la-chee' (ant), 'be-la-sana' (apple) and 'tse-nill' (axe) all stood for the letter 'a'. The following table shows some of the Navajo words used for each letter:

A	Ant	Wol-la-chee	N	Nut	Nesh-chee
B	Bear	Shush	O	Owl	Ne-ahs-jsh
C	Cat	Moasi	P	Pig	Bi-sodih
D	Deer	Be	Q	Quiver	Ca-yeilth
E	Elk	Dzeh	R	Rabbit	Gah
F	Fox	Ma-e	S	Sheep	Dibeh
G	Goat	Klizzie	T	Turkey	Than-zie
H	Horse	Lin	U	Ute	No-da-ih
I	Ice	Tkin	V	Victor	A-keh-di-glin
J	Jackass	Tkele-cho-gi	W	Weasel	Gloe-ih
K	Kid	Klizzie-yazzi	X	Cross	Al-an-as-dzoh
L	Lamb	Dibeh-yazzi	Y	Yucca	Tsah-as-zih
M	Mouse	Na-as-tso-si	Z	Zinc	Besh-do-gliz

After their training, the code talkers were put to the test and passed easily. A series of messages translated into Navajo, transmitted via radio, and translated back into English again were found to be word-perfect.

The renowned Navy Intelligence unit was then given a chance to crack the code, but after three weeks they were stumped. The Navajo language was a 'weird succession of guttural, nasal, tongue-twisting sounds', they said. 'We couldn't even transcribe it, much less crack it.'

The code was deemed a success, and by August 1942 a group of 27 code talkers had landed on Guadalcanal, where the US and its allies were waging a brutally hard campaign against the Japanese. They were the first of 420 Navajo code talkers who participated in every assault the US Marines conducted between 1942 and 1945 in territories including Guam, Iwo Jima, Okinawa, Peleliu, Saipan, Bougainville and Tarawa.

The Navajo signalmen played a vital role. At Iwo Jima, Major Howard Connor, 5th Marine Division signal officer, had six Navajo code talkers working around the clock during the first two days of the battle. Those six sent and received more than 800 messages, all without error. Major Connor declared, 'Were it not for the Navajos, the Marines would never have taken Iwo Jima.'

In fact, the Navajo code remained impenetrable to Japanese code-breakers. At the end of the war, Japan's chief of intelligence, Lieutenant General Seizo Arisue, admitted that while the Japanese military had broken the US Air Force code, they had made no headway on the Navajo code.

The story of the Navajo code talkers is now known across the world, but until 1968, they and their code remained secret in the interests of US national security. Finally, in 1982, the US government honoured them by naming 14 August 'National Navajo Code Talkers'

Above: The Navajo code.

Day.' The original code talkers received the Congressional Gold Medal, and subsequent code talkers received the Congressional Silver Medal.

THE COLD WAR CODE WAR

The beginnings of the Cold War were already emerging during the Second World War, despite the United States and the USSR being allies.

In early 1943, the SIS instituted a secret program of surveillance on Soviet diplomatic communications, based at Arlington Hall in the state of Virginia. The program, called Venona, was started by a former schoolteacher, Miss Gene Grabeel. When the war ended, Grabeel was joined by the linguist Meredith Gardner, who had worked on some of the German and Japanese codes during the war and was to became Venona's principal translator and analyst for the next 27 years.

It became clear that each of the messages handled by Venona was encrypted using one of five different systems, depending on their sender. The KGB, the Soviet Army General Staff Intelligence Directorate, Soviet Naval Intelligence, diplomats and trade representatives each used a different system.

Lieutenant Richard Hallock, a former archaeologist, was the first to break a message sent by trade representatives. The following year, another cryptanalyst, Cecil Phillips, gained a fundamental insight into the encryption system used in the KGB messages, but it would take another two years of intense cryptanalysis before messages could be read.

All of the cipher schemes used by the Soviets involved double encryption. The first layer of encryption was the replacement of words and phrases by a series of numbers from a code book.

To garble the message further, random numbers taken from a printed pad, of which both the sender and recipient had copies, were added to the message. If these 'one-time' pads had been used by the Soviets correctly – once only, rather than reused several times – the

messages are likely to have remained unbroken. But the fact that some of the one-time pads had duplicate pages, and that these fell into the Allies' hands, gave the cryptanalysts at Arlington Hall a way into the KGB's messages.

Above: Second World War B24 Liberator Bomber over the island of Iwo Jima in the Pacific, on 23 December 1944.

One message deciphered by the Venona cryptanalysts towards the end of 1946 listed the names of the scientists who had worked on the Manhattan atomic bomb project. Many believe that this, and other information about the atomic bomb, enabled the Soviets to develop their own weapons much more quickly and more cheaply than they would otherwise have done – a crucial development in the chilling of relations between the two superpowers.

The 3,000 or so Venona messages were littered with cover names to hide the identity of Soviet spies, as well as other persons and places, such as:

Code name	Real name
KAPITAN	President Roosevelt
BABYLON	San Francisco
ARSENAL	US War Department
THE BANK	US Department of State
ENORMOZ	The Manhattan Project/A-bomb

Below: David Greenglass (left) and Julius Rosenberg (right) arriving at court to be sentenced for their part in a spy ring.

Much of what was revealed in the Venona messages gave the United States information on KGB tradecraft – the practical methods used in espionage and counter-espionage, such as the use of bugging devices.

One Soviet agent turned up by Venona was Julius Rosenberg, who was executed in the US in 1953 with his wife, Ethel, after being convicted of charges of espionage relating to national security. Their conviction and execution have always been controversial. The pair were convicted on evidence from Ethel's brother, David Greenglass, who had worked at the Los Alamos laboratory and said he had passed classified information to his sister and her husband, who then passed it on to the Soviets. Greenglass was identified in Venona messages with the codename Calibre.

Above: The National Secutiry Agency at Fort George Meade, Maryland. Below: The NSA logo.

However, many considered Greenglass's evidence flimsy and questioned the extent of Ethel Rosenberg's involvement. Indeed, when Venona's messages were finally made public in 1995, they gave no information that implicated Ethel, although they did reveal Julius' involvement under his codenames Antenna and Liberal.

The year 1952 saw the establishment of America's National Security Agency (NSA) by President Harry Truman, bringing together the cryptology services of the individual armed services. Originally, its headquarters were to be at Fort Knox in Kentucky, more famous for its gold bullion reserves, but it was eventually based at Fort Meade, Maryland, where it remains to this day.

In the 1950s, cryptanalysis in the United States took something of a back seat with regard to current intelligence, thanks to an increasing reliance on defectors. However, Venona continued its work on the wartime messages until 1980, and many of the Soviet agents uncovered during the 1960s and 1970s were found because of ongoing work by Venona. Only in 1995 were all the 3,000 messages handled by Venona made public, revealing the role of cryptanalysis in the Cold War.

CHAPTER FIVE

S PEED

In today's electronic era, powerful digital encryption
protects data against criminals.
Public-key encryption, factorisation and the Data Encryption Standard.

Criminals often turn to codes and ciphers to hide the nature of their activities. Over the past century, law enforcement authorities have had to become specialists in codebreaking in order to keep one step ahead of those subverting the law. Yet the potential of huge financial rewards have spurred criminals to advance from simple ciphers to highly sophisticated technologies in order to maintain secrecy around their illegal activities.

At the same time, legitimate businesses that use communication channels to carry out transactions, such as Internet banks and online e-tailers, have had to turn to cryptology to keep their customers' financial details secret. In turn, hackers and criminals are also turning their hands to cryptanalysis in an effort to divert some of the billions of pounds worth of money floating around the globe into their own bank accounts.

THE KEY SWAP PROBLEM

With methods of encrypting messages that are virtually or totally impossible to crack, why would anyone want to use a lesser method of   Opposite: Fibre-optic cable

Right: GCHQ
(Government
Communications
Headquarters), one of the
United Kingdom's
intelligence organisations.

encryption? The answer is that very secure encryption systems like these may not be practical in a real-life situation. If encryption takes too much time, then you may need to choose a method that trades security for speed.

Another problem facing anyone trying to send an encrypted message is how to let the recipient know how the message was encrypted in the first place. For ciphers like the alphabetic substitution cipher, the problem is that once the encryption scheme is known by an eavesdropper, all subsequent messages can be easily read.

A system called public-key encryption (PKE) addresses both issues. However, it actually uses two keys: one that is made public, and another that is kept secret. Both keys are issued by a recognised certification authority. The public key is held in the form of an electronic certificate in a directory and is accessible by anyone who wants to communicate with its holder. Both the public key and private key are essentially large numbers that are mathematically related. What this means is that either can be used to encrypt the message, as long as the other key is used to decrypt it.

The first work on PKE was carried out in the early 1970s by James Ellis, Clifford Cocks and Malcolm Williamson at Britain's Government Communications Headquarters (GCHQ), the organisation that grew out of the work of Bletchley Park. Yet, the work was considered so secret that it was only finally made public in 1997.

In the meantime, the idea was independently conceived by Whitfield Diffie and Martin Hellman at Stanford University in the US, and as a result is sometimes known as Diffie-Hellman encryption.

However, knowing that they are mathematically related is not enough of a clue for a would-be codebreaker, since deriving one from the other is considered so difficult as to be virtually impossible. Symmetric ciphers are those that use the same key to encrypt and decrypt, a simple alphabetic substitution for example. Thus, the process of using different keys to encrypt and decrypt the message means that the cipher is known as asymmetric.

One of the major advantages of PKE is that there is no need to have a central database against which to verify the keys, reducing the chances that the key will be intercepted during the verification process by eavesdroppers bugging your communication channel.

MAKING P.K.E. WORK IN THE REAL WORLD

Although the work at GCHQ and Stanford laid the foundations for PKE, a breakthrough in making it suitable for practical use came with the work of Ronald Rivest, Adi Shamir and Leonard Adleman, three researchers at the Massachusetts Institute of Technology. This trio found a mathematical method that could easily be used to relate the public and private keys, but also additionally allow the swapping of digital signatures – a way of confirming the identity of the sender electronically. Their method involved factors and prime numbers.

For any given number, its factors are those whole numbers that divide into it exactly without leaving a remainder. For example, the factors of the number 6 are 1, 2, 3 and 6, since 6 divided by each of these numbers leaves a whole number without a remainder. The number 4 is not a factor of 6, since 6 divided by 4 is 1 with a remainder of 2.

A prime number is a number that only has two factors – itself and the number 1. We can see straight away that the number 6 does not fall into this category, since it has four factors. By contrast, the number 5 is only exactly divisible by itself and 1, and is therefore a prime number.

With this definition in mind, we can write out a list of the first few prime numbers – 2, 3, 5, 7, 11, 13, 17, 19, 23, 29, 31. The number 1 is not considered to be prime since it only has one factor. Multiplying the two largest of the above list of prime numbers – 29 x 31 – is very quick. It is a trivial thing on a calculator, taking seconds. You could probably do it moderately quickly with a pencil and paper, and even not take too much time over it in your head if you took the shortcut of working out 30 x 31 and then subtracting 31 to get 899.

But looking at the problem the other way round, it is considerably more difficult. If you were given the number 899 and asked what its two factors were, it might take an hour with a calculator, a day with pencil and paper and a week in your head.

As the prime numbers involved get larger, the time it takes to work out takes longer and longer. The two largest prime numbers discovered to date have more than seven million digits each. Although this means that multiplying them together is not something your average desktop calculator can do, with a small amount of computing power, you can work it out. Doing the reverse is almost unimaginably time-consuming. However, as with any challenge, there are people who are willing to try. At present, some very large numbers are taking 30 years' worth of computer time to factorise (see Cracking PKE below).

This mathematical fiddling with prime numbers is the basis of what Rivest, Shamir and Adleman came up with. The company the trio formed, RSA Security, now estimates that there are more than a billion implementations of the RSA encryption standard in use in applications today. One popular RSA application helps identify users who wish to have remote access to a corporate IT system. A user logs into their corporate system using a virtual private network, a sort of electronic secure tunnel. Each user is provided with a small fob containing a liquid crystal display. On the display, a six-digit number appears, changing every 30 seconds. To access their system, the user calls up a log-in page and enters a numeric code that identifies him, adds the six digits currently showing on the fob screen, and then types in a pre-arranged password. With this combination, a company can be almost certain that the person logging in is who he says he is.

THE ZODIAC KILLER

WANTED

SAN FRANCISCO POLICE DEPARTMENT

A serial killer publishing a coded letter in a newspaper which, if decrypted, would give clues to his identity sounds like something from the plot of a B movie. Yet this is exactly what happened in real life in the 1960s and 1970s in California's Bay Area.

At least seven murders are believed to have been committed in the area by the same person. Some believe the killer's death-toll could have been in the high 30s.

The killer's connection with ciphers came from a series of correspondence with local newspapers in the area. In 1969, the killer sent three ciphers to the *San Francisco Chronicle*, the *Vallejo Times-Herald* and the *San Francisco Examiner*, which he or she claimed would explain the motives behind the murders.

The cipher, which became known as the three-part cipher, contained around 50 different symbols, some of them similar to those used to represent signs of the Zodiac. As a result, the killer became known as the Zodiac killer.

Because the cipher used more than 26 symbols, it was therefore not based on a simple substitution. However, teacher Donald Harden and his wife managed to crack the message in a few hours. The plaintext is revealed under the coded message:

I like killing people because it is so much fun it is more fun than killing wild game in the forest because man is the most dangerous animal of all to kill something gives me the most thrilling experience it is even better than getting your rocks off with a girl the best part of it is that when I die I will be reborn in paradise and those I have killed will become my slaves I will not give you my name because you will try to slow down or stop my collecting of slaves for afterlife

The ciphertext also included a further 18 characters that appeared to have been encrypted using the

This is the Zodiac speaking

I have become very upset with the people of San Fran Bay Area. They have <u>not</u> complied with my wishes for them to wear some nice ⊕ buttons. I promiced to punish them if they didnot comply, by anilating a full School Bass. But now school is out for the summer, so I panished them in an another way. I shot a man sitting in a parked car with a .38.

⊕ -12   SFPD-0

The Map coupled with this code will tell you where the bomb is set. You have untill next Fall to diy it up. ⊕

C ∆ J I ■ O K ⅃ A M ꟿ ∆ Ω O R T G
X O F D V ꝟ ◩ H C E L ⊕ P W ∆

Opposite: The 'Wanted' poster put out for the Zodiac killer.
Above: One of the letters written by the Zodiac killer, and a map showing where the killing would take place.

same method. In cracking the cipher, the couple had assumed that the killer would have egotistically started the message with 'I', and that the message would contain the words 'kill' or 'killing'. As you can see, they were proven correct.

It turned out that the three-part cipher was a homophonic cipher, as described in detail in Chapter 1. These use several ciphertext characters to represent each character in the plaintext in order to thwart a codebreaker who intends to use frequency analysis.

The killer continued to send letters to local newspapers, some of which also contained ciphers and which remain uncracked. One was supposed to show the killer's name in ciphertext.

The most famous of the unsolved ciphers is the so-called 340 cipher, so-named because it contains 340 characters.

The ciphertext contains 63 different characters, meaning that it is not a simple monoalphabetic substitution cipher, which would only include 26 different characters. While several people claim to have solved the 340 cipher using a poly-alphabetic approach, none of the solutions proposed so far has been widely accepted. Code-breakers who have tackled the 340 cipher have tried numerous approaches to crack it. Complex statistical analysis looking at the repetition of characters in each individual row and column has led some cryptanalysts to believe that the 340 cipher has been encrypted using a similar scheme to the three-part cipher, but with some words of the plaintext written out backwards.

Communications from the killer ceased without warning in 1974. The killer has never been found or definitively identified.

EXAMPLE OF PUBLIC-KEY ENCRYPTION

Here is a very simplified example of how PKE works. We start by choosing two prime numbers, **P** and **Q**. In the real world these numbers would have hundreds of digits, but for the sake of explanation, **P** is 11 and **Q** is 17.

We first multiply **P** and **Q** together, making 181. This number is called the modulus. We then choose a random number, which we will call **E**, between 1 and the modulus, in this case 3.

We then need to find any number **D** so that (**D** x **E**) -1 is evenly divisible by (**P**-1) x (**Q**-1). In our example, multiplying (P-1) and (Q-1) together (i.e. 10 x 16) gives 160. The number 320 is evenly divisible by 160 (i.e. it gives no remainder) so we can find a value of **D** as follows:

If (**D** x **E**) -1 = 320
and we have already chosen **E** to be 3 then
D = 107

In this very simplified example, the value of **D** comes out to be a whole number to make the calculations as easy as possible. Note that this is not the only possible value of **D**, since we could have chosen a different value of **E** or chosen 480 or 640 or countless other numbers instead of 320.

This may sound like some parlour game, but the mathematics make it almost impossible to calculate the value of **D** from **E** or vice versa unless you know the individual values of **P** and **Q**.

Now we get back to our public and private keys. The public key that we share with everyone is actually two numbers - the modulus (**P** x **Q**) and the number **E**, i.e. 181 and 3 in our example. The private key is the number **D**, 107 in our example. It may seem surprising, given that we do not want to give away the individual values of **P** and **Q**, that we tell every-one the modulus (**P** x **Q**), but this is really at the heart of this technique. Given large enough values of **P** and **Q**, working them out by factorising the modulus would take almost an eternity.

We then use these keys to encrypt and decrypt characters in a message. Let us number the letters of the alphabet so that **A** = 1 and **Z** = 26. To encrypt any particular character, we perform some more calculations on it. Let's say we want to encrypt the letter **G**, the seventh letter, so we work using the number 7.

First we calculate 7 to the power of **E**. 'To the power of' is mathematical shorthand for saying multiply the same thing together **E** times, so 7 to the power of 2 is 7 x 7 = 49, the same as saying 7 squared; 7 to the power of 3 is 7 x 7 x 7 = 343, the same as saying 7 cubed.

We then use something called modular arithmetic, meaning you wrap around after you reach a fixed value, known as the modulus. A good example of modular arithmetic is telling the time, which is effectively modular arithmetic based on the modulus 12 (i.e. five hours after 10 o'clock is not 15 o'clock but 3 o'clock, because after you reach 12 o'clock you reset to zero).

We have already calculated the modulus, the value **P** x **Q**, or 181. The number 343 in modular arithmetic using the modulus 181, is equivalent to 162. That number is the encrypted form of our letter **G**.

So we send the number 162 and our private key **D** – 107 in our case – to the recipient, who does a similar thing to decrypt the message. The recipient calculates 162 to the power of 107, again using the same modular arithmetic. As you can imagine, multiplying 162 together 107 times gives an absolutely enormous number. In fact, it's something like 2 with 236 zeroes after it. But we did it in modular arithmetic, and this would yield the number 7 if we reset the total to zero everytime we reached 181. 7 is the decrypted character – the letter **G**. Our recipient has therefore received the first letter of our message and we can continue in the same way until the whole message is sent securely.

As you can see, even this hugely simplified example is hard to follow, and it certainly needs a powerful computer to do the mathematics. If we had used the sort of numbers used by modern-day encryption software, the mathematics would be impossible without using some of the world's most powerful computers, as we shall see below.

CRACKING POE'S *GRAHAM MAGAZINE* CIPHER

A grounding in mathematics and language helped 27-year-old Gil Broza to unravel a cipher that had stumped codebreakers for more than 150 years.

The cipher first appeared as a challenge in *Graham's Magazine* in December 1841 in an article by code enthusiast and novelist Edgar Allen Poe. Poe had invited readers to submit encrypted texts to the magazine, which he would then solve. By the time the series of articles ended, Poe claimed to have solved them all – although he did not publish their solutions. He finished the series by publishing two ciphers that were supposedly submitted by a Mr W. B. Tyler, and challenged readers to crack them.

The ciphers were forgotten until interest in them was reignited by a theory put forward by Professor Louis Renza of Dartmouth College that W. B. Tyler was none other than Poe himself. In the 1990s, Shawn Rosenheim of Williams College considered this idea further in researching his book *The Cryptographic Imagination: Secret Writing from Edgar Poe to the Internet*.

Spurred on by this research, the first cipher was eventually cracked in 1992, by Professor Terence Whalen, now at the University of Illinois in Chicago. The plaintext turned out to be an extract from a 1713 play by Joseph Addison encrypted using a monoalphabetic substitution cipher.

The decipherment of the first passage focused the attention of codebreakers on the second. In 1998, Rosenheim threw down a challenge to codebreakers to crack the second cipher and put up a $2,500 prize to the person who solved it.

There were thousands of entries, all of which were scrutinised by Rosenheim and two other academics. In July of 2000, Gil Broza submitted a solution, which was not accepted by Rosenheim until October, perhaps, says Broza, 'because they were a little bit in shock that the text was nothing along the lines of what they expected'.

Perhaps surprisingly, Broza is not a native English speaker. He grew up in Israel and only started reading English literature at the age of 14. His first brush with codebreaking came from cryptograms in puzzle magazines. These puzzles are short texts which have been encrypted using a substitution cipher, which can be solved by frequency analysis and by finding word patterns. His love of both mathematics and language led him to study maths and computer science as an undergraduate, going on to complete a masters in computational linguistics.

In solving the cipher, Broza made several assumptions. The first was that the plaintext was in English, a reasonable assumption given that the cipher cracked in 1992 was in English. The second was that the text breaks in the ciphertext corresponded to word breaks in the plaintext. Finally, the repetition of similar looking words, such as aml, anl and aol, in the ciphertext made him believe that it was encrypted using a polyalphabetic substitution cipher. All three assumptions ultimately proved correct.

Broza needed two months of working in the evenings on the cipher to break it. He started by using frequency analysis of both letters and words, a traditional approach used by cryptanalysts, with particular emphasis on trying to find occurrences of the word 'the'. Yet this revealed little. 'I then tried to use computer programs to identify possible candidates for longer words and combinations.' These programs helped by matching groups of non-consecutive cipher-words that shared several characters against word lists found on the Internet, including a list of words used in Scrabble.

'A month later, when those proved to be no help, I decided that the only possible reason was an over-abundance of mistakes, both encryption mistakes and transliteration mistakes, occurring when the printer typeset the probably hand-written cipher. With this confidence that every second or third word was probably misspelled, I decided to be much more lenient with "the" substitutions that didn't look immediately promising.'

This computer-assisted approach yielded some partial words that looked like English, and after much painstaking work, the plaintext was revealed:

It was early spring, warm and sultry glowed the afternoon. The very breezes seemed to share the delicious langour of universal nature, are laden the various and mingled perfumes of the rose and the jessamine, the woodbine and its wildflower. They slowly wafted their fragrant offering to the open window where sat the lovers. The ardent sun shoot fell upon her blushing face and its gentle beauty was more like the creation of romance or the fair inspiration of a dream than the actual reality on earth. Tenderly her lover gazed upon her as the clusterous ringlets were edged by amorous and sportive zephyrs and when he perceived the rude intrusion of the sunlight he sprang to draw the curtain but softly she stayed him. 'No, no, dear Charles,' she softly said, 'much rather you'ld I have a little sun than no air at all.'

'When the decryption was done, my assumption about mistakes was proven – roughly 7 per cent of the characters were wrong,' he says. The word "warm" in the first sentence, for example, was actually decrypted as "warb", while the word "langour" in the second sentence appeared as "langomr". Since the plaintext was a passage from a book, working out the mistakes was relatively easy. What other word could it have been in the first line other than "warm"? If there had been more mistakes, or the plaintext had been a long bank account number, finding those mistakes would have been virtually impossible.

What's the next challenge for Broza? 'I have been looking at the Zodiac cipher and something related to Richard Feynman. I have also looked at the one attributed to Edward Elgar – the letter to Dora [see pages 80–89] – and it totally stumped me. I spent quite a lot of time on it. The thing is, with 87 letters, there's not a whole lot you can do. Another good thing about the Poe cipher is that I had a good sample size to start with.'

Does Broza believe that any code is ever unbreakable? 'Frequency analysis, patterns and matching – those are dead. Encryption is going to be unbreakable unless you find other tricks, like bugging message sources and destinations. I don't think things will be totally unbreakable, but only because they serve human commnunciations and humans make mistakes. Ask any kid who is trying to write his journal in code.'

Above: EFF's Deep Crack machine cracked the first RSA challenge.

CRACKING PKE

As far as codebreakers are concerned, the key to cracking messages encrypted with systems based on PKE is how strong a key the people sending messages to each other have chosen. For encryption based on prime numbers, if two low prime numbers are chosen, it will take relatively little time for a determined would-be cryptanalyst to crack it. However, the encryption used in commercial applications of PKE uses keys that are considerably longer than the trivial example given above.

When you see people talking about 64-bit and 128-bit encryption on the Internet, this refers to the length of the key. A 64-bit (or binary digit) key would have as many as 20 digits. Imagine trying to find the prime factors of the number 44019146190022537727 without a computer. (Before you spend too much time on this, they are 5926535897 and 7427466391.)

Interestingly, the company behind one of the most commonly used encryption systems, RSA Security, runs several challenges with prizes for cryptanalysts. On the face of it, that the company offers up such challenges seems odd. Why should they encourage people to crack their encryption system? In fact, the challenges have a very practical advantage – the company can quickly see how strong their keys need to be to remain secure.

The first of these ongoing challenges focuses on factorisation. When it was launched in 1991, the challenge took the form of factorising ten very large numbers. The first two numbers have already been solved – the first in December 2003, and the second in November 2005. The latter took just over five calendar months to achieve, but would have taken more than 30 years of processing time had the codebreakers not used a network of linked computers to achieve it in the shorter timescale. Of the eight remaining numbers, even the smallest has 174 digits, while the largest has 617. Prizes ranging from $10,000 to $200,000 are offered to the codebreakers who can find their factors.

In setting the challenge, the company says: 'Given the amount of computation required for such a factorisation, the prizes are mainly symbolic. They serve as a small incentive for public demonstrations of factoring on a large scale.'

FINDING FACTORS

Working out the factors of numbers can be done in many ways. Imagine we want to find the factors of the number 12. We can perhaps best visualise this by imagining 12 pebbles.

ooooooooooooo

These 12 pebbles can be evenly divided up in a number of ways:

ooooooooooooo	1 lot of 12
oooooo oooooo	2 lots of 6
oooo oooo oooo	3 lots of 4
ooo ooo ooo ooo	4 lots of 3
oo oo oo oo oo oo	6 lots of 2
o o o o o o o o o o o o	12 lots of 1

These are the only ways of evenly dividing the 12 pebbles, so the numbers to the right of the pebbles indicate the only possible factors of the number 12. The numbers 1 and 12 are called the 'trivial' factors of 12.

In fact, you can do this same process mathematically by dividing the target number by every whole number from 2 upwards, finding all those that leave no remainder – these are the non-trivial factors of the target number. This mathematical technique is known as trial division, and is the most time-consuming method of factorisation as you have to try every number up to half the target number to find all the factors. (You can see that there's no reason to go beyond half the target number as there will always be a remainder other than for the trivial factor of the target number itself.)

To factorise a number like 12 with a group of pebbles or by trial division takes only a few seconds, but doing very large numbers takes a huge amount of time. The sort of numbers that are used as modern day keys have huge numbers of digits and it would take a lifetime to factor them. Thankfully for the codebreaker, there are other methods of factorisation than trial by division, although these typically involve extremely complex mathematics.

THE COMPLEX MATHEMATICS CODEBREAKERS USE TO FACTORISE LARGE NUMBERS

The elliptic curve method is used to factorise numbers of up to 25 digits long. In mathematics, elliptic curves are those that can be represented by the equation:

$$y^2 = x^3 + a x + b$$

Factors are found by using points on these curves and using the mathematics of group theory.

Two methods called the *quadratic* sieve and the *number field* sieve are used for numbers longer than about 50 digits.

The *quadratic* sieve method works by finding a so-called congruence of squares, i.e. two numbers x and y that satisfy the following equation:

$$x^2 = y^2 \bmod n$$

where modn means that we are using modular arithmetic (as described in our box Example of Public Key Encryption) with a modulus of n. To see what this means, if we were working with modulo 12 arithmetic, then if x were 12 and y were 24, this equation would be satisfied.

The equation can then be rewritten as:

$$x^2 - y^2 = 0 \bmod n$$

Using algebra, we are able to rewrite the left-hand side of this equation in a different form:

$$(x=y) \times (x-y) = 0 \bmod n$$

(If you don't believe it, try x = 3 and y = 2. This gives $x^2 = 9$ and $y^2 = 4$ so $x^2 - y^2 = 5$. (x+y) = 5 and (x-y) = 1 and the two multiplied together are again 5.)

This rewritten equation means that among the possible values of x and y, there may be values of (x+y) and (x-y) which when multiplied together give zero in modular arithmetic using modulus n; in other words, there may be two numbers that when multiplied together give the number n, another way of saying that (x+y) and (x-y) are factors of n – exactly the problem we are trying to solve.

There is a trivial example of this using n = 35, x = 6 and y = 1. This gives:

$$x^2 = 36$$
$$y^2 = 1$$
$$x^2 - y^2 = 35$$

In modulo 35 arithmetic, 35 can be written as 0mod35, so this fits our equation. We then calculate x+y to find 7 and x-y to find 5. These two numbers are indeed factors of 35, which you can verify by multiplying them together yourself.

If we therefore choose n to be the number we want to factorise, we can use this technique to look for possible factors, although it will take somewhat longer than our trivial example. The thrill for mathematicians interested in cryptology is the possibility that one day someone will come across a much easier method of finding factors. If they do so, then many of today's encryption techniques will have to be discarded because they will be too easy to crack.

THE DATA ENCRYPTION STANDARD

As well as RSA's factoring challenge, it is also running similar challenges for cryptanalysts to break another encryption system called DES – the Data Encryption Standard. Eight encrypted messages remain unbroken at the time of going to press, with prizes of $10,000 on offer for the lucky codebreaker.

DES has its origins in the early 1970s. It came about because the US National Bureau of Standards (NBS) felt the need for a method of encrypting governmental information that was sensitive, but not top secret. Although the government could have used existing encryption techniques, it asked for proposals for a new encryption system that would, among other requirements, be highly secure, easy to understand, available to everyone, adaptable to a range of situations and cost effective.

None of the submitted ciphers were considered appropriate, and a second request for proposals came in late 1974. This time, an encipherment algorithm proposed by a team at IBM led by Horst Feistel met the criteria.

In 1976, DES was approved for government use and was widely used over the next 25 years. DES is what is known as a block cipher. In this, the message to be encrypted is broken down into blocks of the same fixed length. In the case of DES, these blocks are 64 bits (binary digits) long, the length being chosen because the hardware used at the time handled this length chunks most effectively.

To encrypt a message, the plaintext blocks are subjected to 16 rounds of processing. For each of the 16 rounds, the 64-bit block is divided into left- and right-hand halves, each 32 bits long. A 48-bit long subkey is generated from a secret key initially chosen to encrypt the message.

The right-hand half of the block is then expanded to 48 bits by duplicating some of the binary digits. This is combined with the sub-key for that round using an exclusive-or operation (XOR), which has the properties described in Chapter 4. The resulting 48-bit number is then divided into eight blocks of six binary digits. Each of these eight blocks then passes through something called a substitution or S-box to reduce it back down to four bits. Each of the eight S boxes is different.

S-BOX OUTPUT

If the six-digit input is 011011, then we can find the output from the fifth S box from the following table. The middle four bits of the input are 1101, so we scan down that column and look across the row where the outer bits are 01. The output from the S-box is highlighted, 1001.

	Middle bits															
	0000	0001	0010	0011	0100	0101	0110	0111	1000	1001	1100	1011	1100	1101	1110	1111
Outside 00	0010	1100	0100	0001	0111	1100	1011	0110	1000	0101	0011	1111	1101	0000	1110	1001
bits 01	1110	1011	0010	1100	0100	0111	1101	0001	0101	0000	1111	1100	0011	**1001**	1000	0110
10	0100	0010	0001	1011	1100	1101	0111	1000	1111	1001	1100	0101	0110	0011	0000	1110
11	1011	1000	1100	0111	0001	1110	0010	1101	0110	1111	0000	1001	1100	0100	0101	0011

Thus, we get out eight blocks of four digits, which are strung back together to get a 32-bit-long number. This new number is then combined with the left-hand half of the original using the exclusive-or operation. The left- and right-hand halves are now switched over, and we start on the next round. Eventually, all 16 rounds are completed and the original input has been completely jumbled. Without knowing the original key, decrypting the message is virtually impossible. Or is it?

In 1998, in response to concerns that DES was close to being broken, the National Institute of Standards and Technology (the successor to the NBS) suggested a new standard called Triple DES, a system that involves using DES three times in succession. In 2002, a further enhancement called the Advanced Encryption Standard was released.

Attempts to break DES typically focus on what are known as brute force attacks. Under the DES scheme, the key used to encrypt the plaintext is 56 bits long. Binary digits can have the value zero or one, which means that the DES system has

2^{56} – or 72,057,594,037,927,936 – possible keys. Checking those by hand would be unfeasible, and even using a PC would take an eternity.

As with any code, people have been trying to break DES ever since it was first released. At first, cryptanalysts designed imaginary computers they believed would be able to crack DES. They showed that DES wasn't invincible, and that computers could be built – given enough money and time – to crack it.

The first real rather than virtual DES cracker was put together by a team led by Rocke Verser, a programmer from the mountain town of Loveland in Colorado. Rather than building a single machine to crack DES, he wrote software that could make use of the spare processing power of computers all over the Internet. In 1997, the system broke RSA's first DES challenge in just 96 days.

The following year, the Electronic Frontier Foundation spent a quarter of a million dollars building a machine called DES Cracker containing more than 1,500 chips specially designed for the purpose. It cracked DES in just two days.

Both of these attacks on DES used brute force – trying every possible key until the correct one was found. Techniques for breaking DES by other than brute force have also been demonstrated, such as differential cryptanalysis, and have the potential to break DES without having to check every key.

Differential cryptanalysis works by analysing a very large number of plaintexts and their corresponding DES-encrypted ciphertexts with a computer to see if there are statistical patterns that could reveal the initial key used. However, the number of messages required is still dauntingly high, and breaking it with this method is certainly not trivial.

As a result of very long keys used in public-key encryption (PKE) and the increasingly complex mathematical methods that are needed to find them, modern-day codebreaking is now mostly beyond the realm of the interested amateur and is instead the preserve of mathematicians. But the tantalising possibility remains that there might be a chink in the armour of encryption systems that use the difficulty of factorising large numbers. Although the factorisation methods that have been discovered so far are mathematically complex, a simpler way may still exist.

After all, the mathematics involved in Einstein's theory of relativity is horribly complex, yet out of the complexity came the beautifully simple equation E=mc². Thus, codebreakers around the world are focusing their efforts on finding simple factorisation methods. If they do find them, encrypting messages using public-key encryption, RSA or DES will be as secure as using Caesar's alphabetic shift.

MAKING THE INTERNET SECURE

Although many of the messages we send via email are trivial, there are times when we want to make sure that no-one can snoop on what we are saying. If you are applying for a new job, for example, the last thing you want is for your existing employer to find out.

One way of encrypting emails is to use a software package known as Pretty Good Privacy (PGP), which combines elements of conventional cryptography and public-key encryption. PGP was created by Philip R. Zimmermann, and was offered free on the Internet discussion group Usenet in 1991. The PGP software generates a random key based on the movements of your mouse and the way you type. This random key is then used to encrypt your message.

The next stage is to use public-key encryption, but instead of using this to encrypt the message, the random key used in the previous stage is encrypted using your public key and sent along with the message which has been encrypted using the random key. When the recipient receives your message, instead of using the private key to decrypt the message, they decrypt the random key, and then use that to decrypt the attached message.

The publication of PGP on Usenet saw Zimmermann subject to a criminal investigation by the US government which claimed that publishing PGP in this way violated US export restrictions for cryptographic software. The restrictions were put in place because the US government wants to restrict universal access to strong cryptographic techniques. Although the cryptanalysts at the National Security Agency can without a doubt decrypt anything that has been encrypted with the PGP software using a short binary key, it is

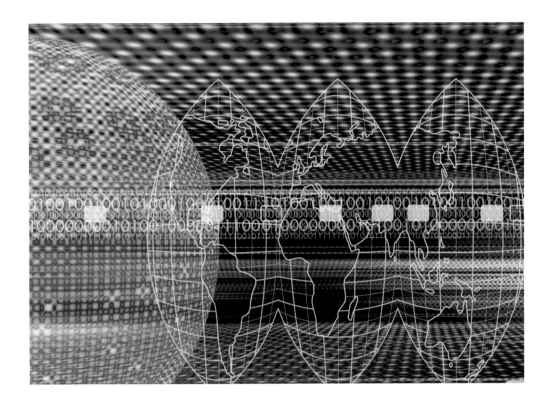

uncertain whether it can break messages encrypted using very long keys. The US government dropped its case in January 1996, although the Attorney General declined to comment on its reasons for doing so.

Encryption is also used when you visit 'secure' websites. They can be identified by the appearance of a small padlock symbol in the bottom right of your browser window, and also by web addresses beginning with https instead of http. Sites such as this use a technology called Secure Sockets Layer, or SSL In fact, SSL uses public key encryption as described previously, typically with keys that are 128 binary digits long, to secure the connection between you and the computer you are talking to. The codebreaker wanting to hack into your bank account details, for example, faces the same challenges as codebreakers trying to crack messages sent using the same encryption scheme.

Above: PGP and SSL offer Internet and email security for all data worldwide.

CODES IN FICTION

53++!305))6*;4826)4+.)4+);806*;48!8`60))
85;]8*:+*8!83(88)5*!;46(;88*96*?;8)*+(;4
85);5*!2:*+(;4956*2(5*−4)8`8*;4069285);)6
!8)4++;1(+9;48081;8:8+1;48!85;4)485!52880
6*81(+9;48;(88;4(+?34;48)4+;161;:188;+?;

Above: The coded message in Edgar Allen Poe's *The Gold Bug*.
Opposite: Arthur Conan Doyle (1859–1930), author of the Sherlock Holmes mysteries.

The American novelist Edgar Allen Poe was fascinated by codes and ciphers. The plot of one of his most famous stories, *The Gold Bug*, centred on a coded message found on a scrap of parchment.

One of the protagonists uses the techniques of frequency analysis to decode the message (see below), which appears to give directions to a treasure hoard buried by a pirate named Kidd:

'*A good glass in the bishop's hostel in the devil's seat forty-one degrees and thirteen minutes northeast and by north main branch seventh limb east side shoot from the left eye of the death's-head a bee-line from the tree through the shot fifty feet out.*'

The Gold Bug was not Poe's only writing on codes. Between 1839 and 1841, he wrote extensively about codes in the Philadelphia newspaper *Alexander's Weekly Messenger*, and the periodical *Graham's Magazine*, and asked his readers to send him ciphers, which he would crack. He wrote: 'Let this be put to the test. Let anyone address us a letter in this way, and we pledge ourselves to read it forthwith – however unusual or arbitrary may be the characters employed.'

Poe received a considerable amount of mail from this request, and published many of the solutions in his columns, although he never revealed how he had cracked them. Yet the story line of *The Gold Bug*, published in 1843, may give some clues as to how he achieved it.

Poe used his last article in *Graham's Magazine* to challenge his readers to crack two ciphers, purportedly sent by a Mr W. B. Tyler. It took over 150 years for them to be solved (see pages 136–137).

In Arthur Conan Doyle's *Adventure of the Dancing Men*, Sherlock Holmes is challenged to solve codes using the same system. In the novel, a Norfolk squire takes an American wife, who makes him promise never to ask her about her life before coming to Britain. After a year or so of marriage, the squire's wife receives a letter from America which visibly shocks her, but which she throws into the fire. Soon afterwards, a series of messages made up of dancing stick men appears scrawled on walls and left on scraps of paper about the country house, which again appears to make the squire's American wife uncomfortable. Having promised not to question his wife on the matter, the squire approaches Holmes to unravel the secrets of these messages. After receiving several messages, Holmes heads to Norfolk in a hurry, but arrives to discover that the squire has been shot dead and the wife seriously wounded.

Like Legrand in *The Gold Bug*, Holmes employs frequency analysis to decode the messages. Unlike Legrand, Holmes has several messages, which he can use to uncover the cipher, and his job is made easier by the use of the flags shown, which Holmes deduces indicate the word breaks. The multiple messages also give him enough characters to use frequency analysis and decipher the first message. It reads: 'Am here Abe Slaney'.

Holmes discovers that an American by the name of Abe Slaney is staying at a nearby farm and sends a message to him using the same code. Slaney turns out to be the former fiancé of the squire's wife, and a gangster whose gang had created the dancing men code.

Another Holmes adventure – *The Valley of Fear* – sees the detective receive a coded message as follows:

534C21312736314172141
DOUGLAS109293537BIRLSTONE
26BIRLSTONE947171

Holmes works out that the C2 in the first refers to the second column, while 534 refers to the page number of a specific book. The numbers then indicate a particular word in that column. The sender of the message had intended to convey the name of the book in a second message but changes his mind. Holmes nevertheless works out that the book used as the key to the message is the *Whitaker's Almanac*, and deciphers the message:

There is danger may come very soon one. Douglas rich country now at Birlstone House Birlstone confidence is pressing.

Neal Stephenson's *Cryptonomicon* blends codebreaking fact and fiction. The novel's action centres on Detachment 2702, an Allied unit in the Second World War whose job it is to break Axis codes. Its members include the fictional cryptanalyst Lawrence Waterhouse, morphine-addicted marine Bobby Shaftoe and real-life cryptanalyst Alan Turing. A second strand of the story moves the action to the modern day and sees the descendants of the earlier codebreakers striving to establish a secure international data haven in the fictitious sultanate of Kinakuta.

Ken Follett's *The Key to Rebecca* is based on a true story. Follet explains: 'There was a spy ring based on a house boat in Cairo in 1942 which involved a belly dancer and a British major she was having an affair with. The information at stake was crucial to the battles going on in the desert.'

The coding system used in the *Key to Rebecca* uses a one-time pad (as discussed in Chapter 4) to encrypt a message.

Imagine you wanted to encrypt the message 'The British attack at dawn'. You then choose another chunk of text, which the recipient is made aware of, as a key to encrypt the message. For example, we might choose 'All work and no play makes Jack a dull boy' as our key. We proceed by writing the position of the letters in each underneath the two messages, as shown below, and then add those numbers together. Where the sum is greater than 26, we subtract 26, and then convert the resultant numbers back into their corresponding letters (see below).

Thus, the encrypted message reads Utqx-gaetvehiqolzgelag. The recipient knows the key that was used and is able to decrypt the message by repeating the process in reverse. Even if the message is intercepted, an eavesdropper would need to know the key to decipher it. In Follett's novel, the key was text from Daphne du Maurier's famous novel *Rebecca*.

Novelist Dan Brown has a deep interest in codes. His novel *Digital Fortress* revolves around the National Security Agency, a fictitious computer called TRANSLATR, which can break any cipher, and the events that unfold when TRANSLATR comes up against something it cannot decrypt. The ciphertext is not revealed in the novel, but there are ominous hints of encryption techniques such as rotating cleartexts and mutation strings, which are never explained in full enough detail for the serious cryptanalyst.

Original	T	h	e	B	r	i	t	s	h	a	t	t	a	c	k	a	t	d	a	w	n
Position in alphabet	20	8	5	2	18	9	20	19	8	1	20	20	1	3	11	1	20	4	1	22	14
Key	A	l	l	w	o	r	k	a	n	d	n	o	p	l	a	y	m	a	k	e	s
Position in alphabet	1	12	12	22	15	18	11	1	14	4	14	15	16	12	1	25	13	1	11	5	19
Sum (less 26 if greater than 26)	21	20	17	24	7	1	5	20	22	5	8	9	17	15	12	26	7	5	12	1	7
Encrypted letter	U	t	q	x	g	a	e	t	v	e	h	i	q	o	l	z	g	e	l	a	g

On the endpapers of the book is an interesting challenge for budding cryptanalysts. It is a series of numbers as follows:

128-10-93-85-10-128-98-112-6-6-25-126-39-1-68-78

To solve it, you need to arrange the numbers in a four by four block with the numbers running downwards:

128	10	6	39
10	128	6	1
93	98	25	68
85	112	126	78

The numbers then refer to chapters within the book. The first letter of the corresponding chapter then replaces each number to give the message 'We are watching you'.

Perhaps the most famous appearance of code-breaking in fiction in recent years occurs in one of Dan Brown's other novels, *The Da Vinci Code*. In the book, Harvard symbologist Robert Langdon cracks a series of codes linked to the works of Leonardo da Vinci. Langdon finds a three-line message written in blood next to the murdered body of a curator at the Louvre in Paris:

13-3-2-21-1-1-8-5

O, draconian devil!

Oh, lame saint!

Langdon and a French cryptographer Sophie Neveu work out that the second and third lines are anagrams of 'Leonardo da Vinci' and 'The

Above: Leonardo Da Vinci's *Mona Lisa*, one of the clues in Dan Brown's *The Da Vinci Code*.

Mona Lisa' respectively. A message scrawled in pen on the Mona Lisa – only visible in ultraviolet light – then leads them on a whistlestop tour of the globe as they try to discover why the curator was murdered.

The line of figures turns out to be a series of numbers called Fibonacci numbers, which are also the access code to a Swiss bank account.

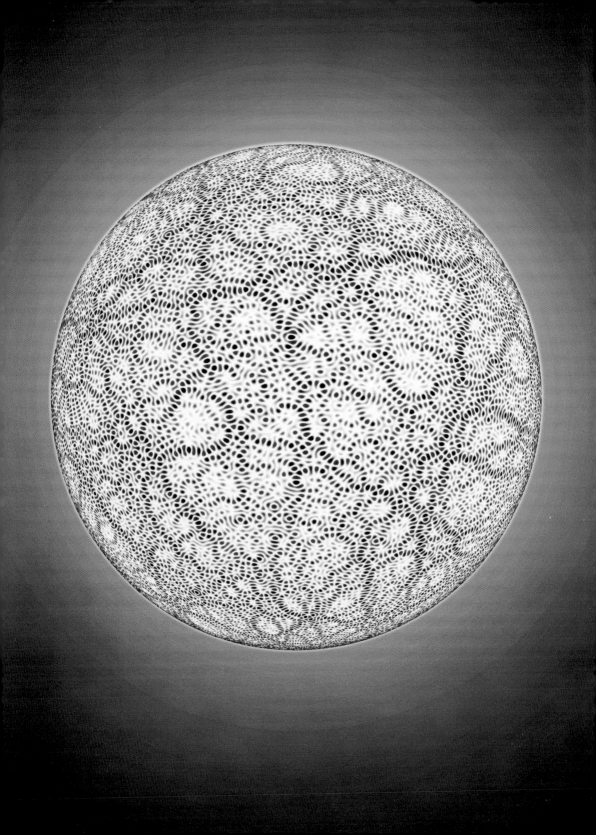

CHAPTER SIX

VISION

Quantum cryptography is touted as being uncrackable;
will it mean the end of codebreakers?
Crypto moves into the realms of quantum physics and chaos theory.

One sunny afternoon in October 1979, a young Canadian computer scientist, Gilles Brassard, was enjoying a dip in the balmy waters of a hotel beach on the island of Puerto Rico, when a complete stranger unexpectedly swam up and launched into a conversation about quantum physics.

'This was probably the most bizarre, and certainly the most magical, moment in my professional career,' Brassard says. The stranger, it quickly emerged, was Charles Bennett, a scientist from New York who was on the island for the same reason as Brassard – to attend a meeting of the Institute of Electrical and Electronics Engineers. And the watery meeting was far from random. Bennett had specifically wanted to talk to his Canadian colleague because they were both interested in cryptography. Within hours, the two had started working together on some radical new ideas, beginning a collaboration that has changed forever the nature of cryptology.

The concepts Bennett and Brassard came up with on the sand of the Caribbean that fall soon resulted in the publication of the first scientific paper on quantum cryptography, a totally new kind of encryption that is genuinely unbreakable.

Opposite: Computer model showing many quantum wave paths superimposed onto the surface of a sphere, producing a random wave – an example of quantum chaos.

In that sense, quantum cryptography is unique. Every other form
of cryptography invented in the long and tortured history of codes and
ciphers – except, perhaps, cumbersome one-time pads – has been
vulnerable to the skill of codebreakers. The same cannot be said of
quantum cryptography – its perfect security is founded on nothing
less than the laws of physics.

A COMPUTER IN A TEACUP

Quantum physics, also known as quantum mechanics, is an
extremely successful framework for explaining the way the world
works. As the field of physics that deals with what happens at a very,
very small scale, it is the only way to get an accurate mathematical
model of subatomic particle interactions. Nearly a century of
experimental hammering has only confirmed that it is right.

Nevertheless, there's also no denying that the details of quantum mechanics are a little strange. To take just a simple example, in one of the more famous quantum physics experiments a particle of light (known as a photon) was shown to be capable of being in two places at once (see pages 158–159).

The theory might also be difficult to accept because it deals with probabilities, not certainties. Einstein himself had serious doubts about the uncertainty inherent in its calculations. 'Quantum mechanics is certainly imposing. But an inner voice tells me that it is not yet the real thing,' he wrote in a letter to his fellow physicist Max Born in 1926.

Physicist Brian Cox thinks that what makes quantum mechanics so difficult to grapple with is that it quickly raises fundamental questions about why the universe is the way it is. 'The challenge to your common sense is really on the surface with quantum mechanics,' says Cox. 'You don't have to think deeply about it to get to a difficult problem. For most theories the "why" stuff is hidden, but for quantum mechanics you're forced to get into this deeper stuff (such as parallel universes) because it's so strange.'

During the past couple of decades, scientists realised that some of those counterintuitive aspects of quantum mechanics could have enormous ramifications in making more powerful computers. A significant milestone occurred in 1985, just a year after Brassard and Bennett published their paper on quantum computing. In that year, a brilliant scientist from the University of Oxford, David Deutsch, first described a universal quantum computer.

In his book, *The Fabric of Reality*, Deutsch envisaged a computer that did not operate at the level of classical physics, as everyday computers do. Instead, the computer he described functioned at the tiny, quantum level. Deutsch describes quantum computers as machines that use uniquely quantum-mechanical effects to perform types of computation that would be impossible, even in principle, on any classical computer. 'Quantum computation is therefore nothing less than a distinctively new way of harnessing nature,' he wrote.

THE CAT CAME BACK

Above: The 'Schrödinger's Cat' thought experiment, with the cat shown as both alive (ginger) and dead (grey).

In 1935, the brilliant Austrian physicist, Erwin Schrödinger, a Nobel Prize winner, published an article in which he described a hypothetical experiment that is often used to help illustrate the concept of quantum superposition.

In the article, Schrödinger asked his readers to imagine a cat inside a box. Now imagine that also inside the box is an atom that has a 50/50 likelihood of decaying in an hour, a radiation detector and a flask containing poison gas. If the atom decays, the radiation detector will trigger a switch that releases the gas and kills the cat.

Obviously, when the experimenter opens the lid of the box after an hour, the atom will either still be intact or will have decayed, and the cat will be either alive or dead. But quantum superposition states that until the lid is opened, the cat is in two states simultaneously: dead and alive. (Schrödinger didn't mean to suggest that he believed that the dead-and-alive cat would actually exist. Instead, his view was that quantum mechanics was incomplete and not representative of reality, at least in this case.)

However, whatever Schrödinger thought, the idea of superposition isn't mere fantasy. In fact, it is the only possible way to explain many real-world phenomena. For computers, the implications are enormous.

The parts of quantum mechanics that have the most relevance for computers relate to a concept known as *superposition*. This means that any quantum element can be in several different states simultaneously – and only resolves into one or the other when someone examines it.

The phenomenon of quantum superposition means that quantum computers would have unimaginable power, perhaps in a device the size of a tea cup. That's because, while in normal computers the basic unit of information (the bit) exists as either a 1 or a 0, at the miniscule level where quantum mechanics kick in, 'quantum bits' can effectively be in the classical 0 and 1 states at the same time.

This means that a computer operation on a single quantum bit – known as a qubit, and pronounced 'kew-bit' – acts on both of the values at the same time. A qubit might, for example, be represented by an electron in one of two different states – let's call them 0 or 1. But unlike regular bits, qubits can be both 0 and 1 at the same time, thanks to the quantum phenomenon of superposition.

Above: Erwin Schrödinger (1887–1901), the Austrian physicist and Nobel Prize winner who created the 'Schrödinger's Cat' thought experiment described opposite.

So, by performing an operation on one qubit, the computer has actually performed the operation on two different values at the same time. Thus, a system that involved two qubits would be able to perform an operation on 4 values, and so on. As you add qubits, computing power increases exponentially.

Another bizarre property of qubits is known as 'entanglement'. When two or more qubits are entangled, their properties become inextricably linked no matter how far apart they become, in effect wiring them together. This spooky linkage means that when you measure the state of one of the two qubits, the state of the other becomes immediately fixed too – they can be manipulated so that when one is measured to be 1, the other is 0.

Given the massive increase in power that quantum computers offer, governments have realised that they pose an enormous threat to information security. In the 20 years since David Deutsch published his paper on quantum computers, research has reached a frenetic pace around the world, but large-scale quantum computers haven't yet become a reality. However, researchers have begun to figure out how to program them; and interestingly, two of the first applications relate to cryptanalysis.

The first came in 1994, when Peter Shor of Bell Laboratories in New Jersey showed how a quantum machine could be used to crack systems such as RSA, the very widely used cryptographic algorithm that gains its security from the fact that normal computers struggle to 'factorise' very large numbers (see Chapter 5).

According to one estimate, factorising a number with 25 digits would take all the computers on earth centuries to achieve. Using the quantum technique Peter Shor invented, it might take just minutes.

Shor's algorithm, as this technique is known, is remarkably simple and does not need the type of hardware required to build a full quantum computer. As David Deutsch points out, this makes it likely that a quantum factorisation engine will be built long before a full-capacity quantum computer. Two years later, Lov Grover, also from Bell Labs, described another quantum computing algorithm that allowed long lists to be searched extremely quickly, another application of great interest to cryptanalysts.

However, despite these advances, researchers have struggled to turn the theory of quantum computing into full-scale reality. In the late 1990s, the researchers Neil Gershenfeld and Isaac L. Chuang explained why. In an article in *Scientific American* magazine, they pointed out that almost any interaction that a quantum system has with its environment, for example an atom colliding with another atom, constitutes a physical observation. When this happens, quantum superposition collapses into a single definite state, making further quantum calculation impossible. 'Thus, the inner workings of a quantum computer must somehow be separated from its surroundings to maintain coherence,' they explained. 'But they must also be accessible so that calculations can be loaded, executed and read out.'

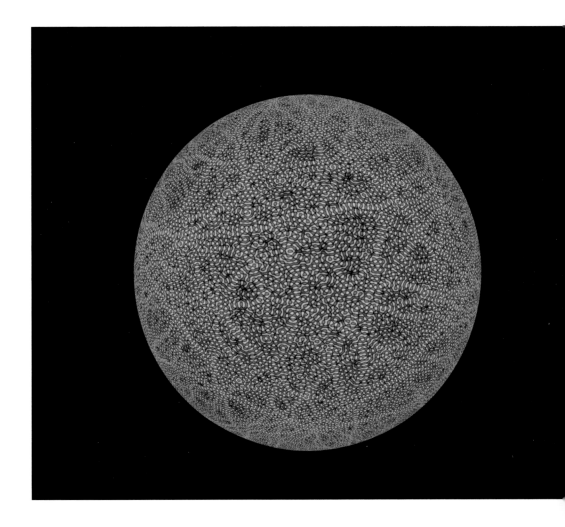

QUANTUM CRYPTOGRAPHY

The practical implementation of quantum computers may be trouble-some, but they are still seen as a potential threat to communication security. Thankfully, researchers and engineers have come to the rescue with their own quantum magic, which can be used to distribute cryptographic keys under the perfect protection of the laws of physics.

Some quantum key distribution systems rely on the fact that individual photons vibrate at different angles as they move through space, a property that scientists refer to as their *polarisation*.

Above: Computer model simulating the motion of a particle that is behaving like a wave. Quantum theory states that as the particle moves it creates many 'wave trains', which can collide to produce one random quantum wave, an example of quantum chaos.

QUANTUM CRYPTOGRAPHY – BEING IN TWO PLACES AT ONCE

In the winter of 1803, a 30-year-old English researcher by the name of Thomas Young stood before some of the world's eminent scientists in London and performed an experiment that would challenge their views on the very nature of the physical world, by showing that light had the properties of a wave.

Young had an exceptional mind. By the age of 14 he had already studied Greek, Latin, French, Italian, Hebrew, Arabic and Turkish, among other languages. At 19 he had begun to study medicine, and four years later had obtained the degree of doctor of physics. He was appointed professor of physics at the Royal Institution in 1801, and in two years had delivered 91 lectures.

Still, the challenge he faced that day in November 1803 was not insignificant, considering that Isaac Newton himself had believed that light was made of tiny bullet-like particles.

To prove his point, Young had an assistant take a mirror outside and stand in front of a window to the room in which his experiment was to take place. A shutter was closed over the window with a pinhole drilled into it so that when the assistant angled the mirror correctly, a thin beam of light shot across the darkened room and hit the wall opposite.

Next, Young took a thin piece of card and carefully placed it so that it cut the beam of light in half. When he did so, the light shining through the window formed a pattern of light and dark stripes on the wall opposite.

'It will not be denied by the most prejudiced,' Young told his audience, 'that the fringes (which are observed) are produced by the interference of two portions of light.' In other words, the pattern of 'fringes' or stripes was caused as light waves interfered with each other as they recombined after being split by the card, much as waves in water recombine to create peaks and swells. In the brighter spots, two 'peaks' in the light wave coincided as they reached the wall, while the darker spots resulted from when a peak and a trough occurred together.

Young later showed the same effect when he shone a thin beam of light at a screen in which

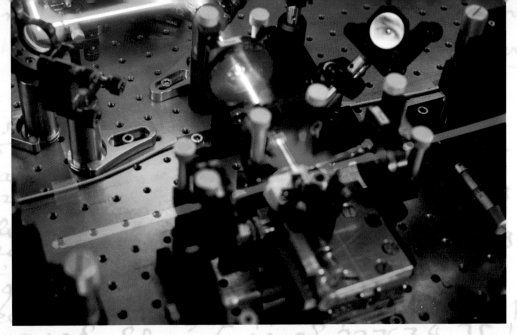

Opposite: Thomas Young (1773–1829). Above: Quantum cryptography equipment.

two slits had been cut, an experiment now known as the 'double-slit experiment'.

These days, scientists know that light has a kind of split personality – behaving like a wave or like a particle, depending on the circumstances. In this context, the result of Young's experiment can be thought of in terms of particles of light – known as photons – interacting after they've passed through the slits.

Thanks to modern technology, scientists are able to repeat Young's experiment using light sources so faint that they only emit one photon of light at a time. When they do this, however, they observe some fascinating results. If, for example, a researcher sets up Young's double-slit experiment using a source of light that sends photons toward the screen at a rate of one per hour, what he finds is that exactly the same pattern of 'interference' gradually appears, even though there is apparently no way any two photons could have interacted. This baffling result can't be explained using the classical laws of physics, but quantum physics has two possible explanations.

The first idea is that the photon in essence passes through both slits at the same time, and subsequently interferes with itself. This comes under the concept of superposition (see page 155).

Another explanation some scientists offer for superposition is referred to as the 'many-worlds' interpretation. In this view, when the single photon reaches the screen in which two slits are cut, it passes through only one of them, but subsequently interacts with another 'ghost' photon that exists in a parallel universe and passed through the other slit.

Either way, the concept of quantum super-position has important implications for quantum computers. Because the elements of a quantum computer can be in multiple states at once, and because it can act on all those different states at the same time, it can perform numerous operations in parallel.

The photons that come out of a normal light source, such as a light-bulb, vibrate in all different directions, but by passing a beam of light through a special filter known as a Polaroid, it is possible to make all the photons in the beam come out of the other side of the filter vibrating in the same direction. This can then be utilised in the field of cryptography.

For the purposes of cryptography, light can be polarised in two ways. The first polarises the vibration of the photon horizontally or vertically, and is known as rectilinear polarisation. The second method makes photons vibrate diagonally, from top-left to bottom-right, or top-right to bottom-left.

These different options can be used as a way of representing the os or 1s of a series of quantum bits. For example, in the rectilinear scheme, horizontal polarisation (-) might represent o, making vertical polarisation (1) represent 1. Alternatively, in the diagonal scheme, left-handed diagonal polarisation (\) might represent o, with right-handed (/) representing 1.

What makes this scheme good for sending secret messages is that, in order for an eavesdropper to correctly measure each photon's vibration, he or she would need to know in advance which polarisation method the sender had used. If a particular photon had been polarised in a rectilinear way, then only a rectilinear detector will accurately tell you whether it is a 1 or a o. If you wrongly use a diagonal detector, then you will wrongly interpret the photon as being either \ or /, and never be the wiser.

The trouble is, simply using this method to send a message leaves the person receiving the message in exactly the same situation as an eavesdropper. Before the person receiving the message can interpret the stream of photons accurately, he or she needs to know what polarisation scheme was used for each photon. Without this information, the message is useless.

To overcome this problem, Brassard and Bennett developed a scheme in which the stream of photons doesn't represent the message – only the key.

It works like this. The person who wants to send an encrypted message – let's call her Alice – sends a series of photons representing 1s and 0s that she has randomly polarised using both the rectilinear and diagonal processes.

Let's imagine Alice sends a series of six photons.

Alice's bit sequence	1	0	0	1	1	0
Polarisation sequence	X	+	X	+	+	X
Photon sent	/	-	\	I	I	\

X= diagonal; += rectilinear

The next step is for Bob – the recipient of the message – to measure the polarisation of the photons once they've reached him. To do this, he randomly swaps between his rectilinear and diagonal polarisation detectors. This means that sometimes his choice will match the choice Alice made, and sometimes it won't.

Alice's bit sequence	1	0	0	1	1	0
Bob's guess of polarisation	X	X	+	+	X	X
Bob's measurement	/	\	-	I	/	\

You can see here that Bob's random choice of detector gave him the right result for three of the photons – the first, fourth and sixth. The trouble is, he doesn't know which of them are right.

To overcome this problem, Alice and Bob simply need to get on the telephone so that she can tell him which polarisation scheme she used for each photon – without revealing whether the bit was 0 or 1.

It doesn't matter whether someone is listening in on this conversation because Alice isn't revealing which bits she sent, only the polarisation scheme she used. Bob can then know for certain that he got it right for photons one, four and six. In this way, Bob and Alice both know for certain what those bits are without discussing them directly. This allows Alice and Bob to use those three photons (in reality they would use many more) as an encryption key whose security is guaranteed by the laws of physics.

The beauty of the system is that if anyone tries to eavesdrop on the exchange, measuring the photons in the wrong mode will introduce the same kind of error that Bob created before Alice told him the correct sequence of polarisation methods.

Quantum key distribution can also make use of 'entanglement', where the properties of two particles rely on each other. In this kind of system – the brainchild of British researcher Artur Ekert – Alice and Bob use pairs of entangled photons to serve as the basis of the key.

Several companies around the world have been developing commercial versions of these systems. Government agencies are also involved, such as the Defence Advanced Research Projects Agency (DARPA), which funded the first continuously running quantum-cryptography network outside a lab, connecting sites in the northeast of the United States, and Europe's 'Secure Communication based on Quantum Cryptography' project.

Dr Andrew Shields, group leader at Toshiba's Quantum Information Group , explains the ultimate security the quantum system offers. 'We could well be coming to the end of the cryptography arms race,' he says. 'As long as the laws of physics hold true, it is totally secure.'

So far, however, distance is proving to be a real limitation for quantum cryptographic systems because of physical problems to do with sending photons long distances down fibre-optic tubes. The longest distances over which quantum keys have been distributed so far are less than 100 kilometres (60 miles), meaning that quantum systems are only good for communications within a city and its surrounding area, for example.

'If you really want to go to 100 kilometres, you would need new technology,' says Nicolas Gisin, a quantum cryptography pioneer from the University of Geneva in Switzerland. An example of such new technology might be a kind of quantum memory that is able to store photons and all the secrets they encode. To send messages longer distances might involve using a kind of relay system that passes messages from one secure location to another.

QUANTUM VULNERABILITY

The laws of physics might ensure the security of keys distributed through quantum channels, but cryptography is only part of the battle when it comes to ensuring data secrecy.

That is, quantum cryptography is not going to protect systems against software or hardware vulnerabilities, or against the sort of human failings that have always left communications systems at risk. An insider job, for example, is hard to stop. And quantum mechanics is going to be of no help if all your secret data is stored on a memory stick and left in the back of a taxi.

Similarly, real-world quantum cryptographic systems also need to include non-quantum parts, and these need to be protected in the usual ways. And an eavesdropper might also try tapping into the optical fibre between Alice and Bob to send an unwanted signal that could overwhelm or damage part of their technology.

Also, as the journalist Gary Stix wrote in an article in *Scientific American* magazine in early 2005, quantum cryptography may also be vulnerable to unusual attacks. 'An eavesdropper might sabotage a receiver's detector, causing qubits received from a sender to leak back into a fibre and be intercepted.'

However, Nicolas Gisin says that new generations of quantum cryptographic systems now being developed can overcome many of these attacks, by incorporating filters that only allow appropriate wavelengths of light into receivers, and by ensuring that Alice and Bob really are talking to one another and not to an eavesdropper pretending to be one or the other of them.

SECRETS IN THE FLAP OF A BUTTERFLY'S WINGS

Quantum cryptography may or may not represent an end to the long battle between cryptographers and cryptanalysts, but in the meantime, new and exotic means of generating secrecy are still being invented. In late 2005, for example, a group of European researchers reported in the scientific journal *Nature* that some of the principles of

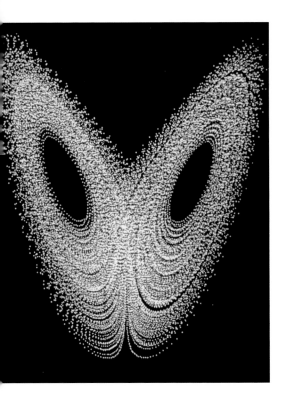

Above: The Lorenz Attractor, a three-dimensional graph produced by chaos mathematics.

chaos theory could be used to keep phone calls secret.

The particular aspect of chaos theory that applies to keeping secrets safe is known as 'the butterfly effect'. This phenomenon got its name in 1972, when scientist Edward Lorenz gave a talk entitled 'Predictability: does the flap of a butterfly's wings in Brazil set off a tornado in Texas?'

Lorenz was illustrating the fact that small variations in the starting conditions of complicated systems, like weather patterns, for example, can produce large variations in the long term. Those changes are so contingent on minute details – such as a wind produced by the flap of a butterfly's wing – that they are largely unpredictable.

The impact of those tiny changes might appear to be random, but that appearance is misleading. Instead, chaotic systems such as the atmosphere, the solar system and economies exhibit patterns, and the different elements of a system – like wind speed and temperature – behave interdependently.

Over the past 20 years or more, scientists have been working on ways to apply the principles of chaos to improve security in communication. The basic idea is that a message could be buried within a chaotic masking signal that would make it inaccessible to anyone who couldn't pierce the chaos.

The trick to extracting messages buried in chaotic background noise is having a receiver that is very well matched to the transmitter that sent the message.

In the *Nature* article, Alan Shore from Free University Brussels, in Belgium, and others, based a system for using these principles on two lasers – one that acted as a transmitter, and another as a receiver.

Under normal circumstances, the light produced by lasers is anything but chaotic, but the researchers created chaos by feeding light back into the laser itself, stimulating it to produce a chaotic mix of different frequencies that are a little like the feedback noise that can be generated by loudspeakers.

Once the message is added to this chaotic mess of light, it is incomprehensible unless it is fed into an identical laser set up in exactly the same way to produce the same pattern of feedback. For this to work, the lasers need to be made with the same equipment and the same components at the same time.

We can think about why this must be the case in terms of the butterfly effect. For the chaotic light being generated by the two lasers to be exactly the same, it needs to have developed from two systems that had exactly the same starting point. In these circumstances, subtracting the chaotic noise from the transmission will reveal the message.

Shore and his colleagues showed for the first time in their *Nature* paper that this kind of system could send secure messages through 120 kilometres (75 miles) of fibre-optic cable around Athens, Greece, raising the possibility that it could be used to make telephone messages more secure. What's more, the transmission rates they can achieve with it are very high – in the kind of range that would make it useful for telecommunications companies. The results also show that the technology can stand up to real-world conditions.

To unravel a message that has been sent bundled in a chaotic carrier signal, an eavesdropper would need to have the means to bleed off some of the chaotic light, and a laser that was precisely matched to the one used to generate the message. The Athens project coordinator, Claudio Mirasso, said in 2005 that 'anyone wanting to break the encryption has to know as much as the people using it, and have a virtually identical device'.

Another expert in the field, Rajarshi Roy, commented when the article was published that the security aspects of chaos-based communications need much further analysis. Nevertheless, he said, they could potentially offer 'privacy in a manner that could be complementary to and compatible with conventional software-based and quantum-cryptographic systems'. That is, messages that have already been encrypted by these other methods could be further obscured courtesy of chaos.

QUANTUM CRYPTOGRAPHY IN A BOX OF CHOCOLATES

The concepts behind quantum cryptography might at first seem complicated, but an Austrian physicist called Karl Svozil has devised a stage show that explains how a system works using actors, two pairs of coloured spectacles – one red and one green – and a bowl of foil-wrapped chocolate balls.

Svozil's inaugural performance took place in October 2005 at the University of Technology in Vienna. On the stage, he arranged two actors, playing the parts of Alice (who sends the message) and Bob (who receives it), and a bowl of chocolates wrapped in black foil.

On each of the chocolates were two stickers:

a red sticker with either a 'o' on it, representing a horizontally polarised photon, or a '1', representing a vertically polarised photon;

a green sticker with either a 'o', representing a right diagonally polarised photon, or a '1', to represent a left diagonally polarised photon.

When the show began, Alice flipped a coin to decide which glasses to wear. Let's say she got the green pair. This represents the polarisation scheme she is using to send that photon.

Alice took a random chocolate ball out of the bowl – remember that each ball has two stickers on it, one green, one red. The green glasses meant she could only see the numbers written on red stickers, and not those written on the green stickers. On a blackboard she wrote down the colour glasses she used, and the number she could see on the chocolate. A member of the audience then took on the role of a photon, shuttling the chocolate ball from Alice to Bob.

Next, Bob flipped a coin to chose a pair of glasses. It doesn't matter which pair he got, but let's say he got the red pair. He took a look at the ball and made a note of what number he could see, and what colour glasses he used. If he used the same colour glasses as Alice, he would see the same number.

After receiving the chocolate, Bob used a red or green flag to tell Alice what colour glasses he used. Alice let Bob know via her own flag what colour her glasses were. At no point did they communicate what symbol was written on the ball. If the colour of their flags matched, they kept the number, otherwise they discarded the entry.

Because Bob only wrote down his numbers if he had used the same glasses as Alice, after the whole process was repeated several times, the two of them had written down an identical series of os and 1s. They compared just a couple of the symbols to make sure an eavesdropper hadn't been listening in, and, finding all was well, they had a perfectly secure random key they could use for a host of cryptographic applications.

The show was a great hit with the non-specialist audience who watched it, Svozil remembers. More importantly, perhaps, they came away from the experience having learned that although the physics behind quantum cryptography is unfamiliar, the procedure itself is as easily digested as a box of chocolates.

FUTURE UNCERTAIN

In the modern age, the field of cryptology is largely in the hands of physicists and mathematicians. Their willingness to publish their findings in scientific journals and at meetings means there is perhaps more information in the public realm about codes and ciphers than ever before.

And yet, most of what is going on is undoubtedly happening behind closed doors, as it always has. Government agencies, such as America's National Security Agency and Britain's General Communications Headquarters, keep information about codebreaking and cryptography under tight wraps, making the prediction of future development a fool's game.

For some, the growing reliance of our digital world on cryptography is already cause for concern. Government control of cryptography could be a danger to civil liberties if it is regulated in a way that ensures authorities can gain access to anyone's personal data, medical records or email.

In this environment, change is likely to be the only constant. The best we can do, then, is to look back at the history of cryptanalysis, and consider the ruins of so many previously 'unbreakable' codes. In the never-ending struggle between cryptographers and cryptanalysts, the hurdles set by one side of the conflict have always been leapt, eventually, by the other.

Perhaps one day, the complexities of large number factorisation, quantum physics and chaos theory will seem as simple to future code-breakers as the Caesar shift does to us. Given all this, it is worth asking the question: have the limits of human ingenuity been reached in the field of secret-keeping?

The only sensible answer is no. The cryptologic arms race, which has stretched across the millennia and taken us from simple ciphers to the distant reaches of modern physics, is probably not over. While there are people with secrets to keep and others who want to expose them, there will always be a demand for that remarkable and shadowy species, the codebreaker.

APPENDIX

CODEBREAKER CHALLENGE

It's now time to put everything you've learned into practice. Over the next four pages you will find a series of challenges. You will need to look back through the book for clues on how to solve each challenge. The answer to each challenge will then give you a clue as to how to solve the next challenge.

To solve the final challenge, you will need to use the answers from all six challenges.

Challenge 1
For help, refer back to Chapter One, Caesar shift.

AXQTGINUGTTSDBINGPCCNXHSTPSGJCWTCRTEGDRAPXBRGNXIP
QDJIIWTHIGTTIHHDBTIDIWTRDBBDCEJAEXIHPCSRGNDJIAXQTGIN
UGTTSDBPCSTCUGPCRWXHTBTCIETDEATPCSHTCPIDGHQTCDIPUU
GXVWITSUANCDIHIPCSHIXUUPBQXIXDCHSTQIXHEPXSIWTLDGSH
DURPTHPGQTUDGTWTUTAALXAADETCIWTCTMISDDG

Challenge 2
For help, refer back to Chapter Two, Vigenère cipher.

HXLNSFSXHMGMQPQYKSRBGYTRWDIHBGHJEYMLVXXZPLLTRHTG
HFOYWFCYKUOTYBRIBZBUVYGDIKHZJMYMLMLIISKWBXCPAITVJT
XVHGMBZHMMWLMDPYHMLIUTJUZMMMWTMZPLLMCJHNLUNY
GXCYBPFEYBKLMYCGKSLMBXTHEZMMLIUBLUYJEEGXHZERNHWJK
BYOUQASWXYUN ZFRREFXSPLHXIHMHJSFWXIH

Challenge 3
For help, refer back to Chapter Three, Union route cipher.

Guard this reveal every great avoided this some cowboy historians straightforward enemy efforts rows the fills turning table need to read their obfuscation that saucy contended for despite just initial you the nonsense up clue first now attacks technique have emptiness

Challenge 4
For help, refer back to Chapter Four, ADFGX cipher.

Three letters dating from the Second World War were recently found at Bletchley Park. They appear to be in some sort of code.

Letter 1
XAGAXDFAFGFAXGDDFFDDADXGGDFAFFDFFAGAXXDAAXFFXGAX
FDFAFGFGDAAFADADAXAAGXAADFDFFGFFAGADXDDDGAAAAFA
AAFXAAAAGAAAGAAFAFFGGFDAFDDFFFDFDAFFFAXFADFDFFDFF
AXXDDFFGAFADFGDXDADAAGAAFDGFGFAA

Letter 2
XAGAXXAXXGAFDGFADFDAFXDFXXFFAFGDAFDFFAFFFDFFDXGFD
XFADFAFADFDDXXFAXAFADADFAAADFFADFDFGAXAXGAADDGAF
GGDGAADAFADAXDAAAFAGXGADDDDDDDAAFAAFDAFDXFAFGF
AFFFXXDAAADFAFGAAXADAFXDDFFAAXAADAAGAAAAFXDFDXX
AFAADDDD

Letter 3
XAGAGXFDFAGDAFDFADDAADAFAXAFADXADGAXFGGDGADGDD
DGXFAAFDAFFGGDDFDAFXDDFDDGAGDADD

Challenge 5

For help, refer back to Chapter Five, PKE.

NCWLCBHOJHKOYMWTSUZJDUSANN
UXRLVVKNRUIQWUWZGVAWZFMZL

Challenge 6

For help, refer back to Chapter Six.

Bob receives a piece of paper through the post showing the following:

A	01000	N	01111
B	01101	O	01011
C	00111	P	11110
D	10111	Q	01100
E	10110	R	10101
F	01110	S	00100
G	11000	T	11011
H	00011	U	10011
I	10010	V	00001
J	10000	W	10001
K	01010	X	01001
L	00010	Y	10100
M	00101	Z	00110

A day later he receives a phone call from Alice, who says:

+XX++ XX++X +X++X +XX++ +X+XX

Bob replies:
+XXX+ XXX+X +XX+X ++X++ +++XX

What key do you need for the final challenge?

The Final Challenge

While browsing through an antique shop recently, we discovered a bundle of correspondence bearing the mark of the German high command. We bought the bundle and took it home. Many of the letters appeared to be concerned with mundane issues, such as stationery orders and requests for leaves of absence, but two letters stood out. One was a yellowed sheet showing the following:

A	00000	I	01000	Q	10000	Y	11000
B	00001	J	01001	R	10001	Z	11001
C	00010	K	01010	S	10010	*	11010
D	00011	L	01011	T	10011	%	11011
E	00100	M	01100	U	10100	£	11100
F	00101	N	01101	V	10101	&	11101
G	00110	O	01110	W	10110	(	11110
H	00111	P	01111	X	10111	)	11111

Another piece of correspondence that caught our attention had several sentences in English at the top, then what appeared to be a section of code, arranged in rows of four letters. The English text read:

The last key you found on your journey here opens every line of this final cipher. Your final destination is the place made up from the initial letters of the six other keywords and this final keyword. In this place, you will find an unbroken code that many have tried, but all have failed. You have come far; maybe you will be the one to break it.

The code read as follows:

C P G C	& % F K	W M G O	£ M M L
R F U J	Q M J F	* * M Y	C P G £
) (T A	C G J F	A G R K	V
C M R J	D A R &	C P C &	
R % H A	) D J £	£ G O O	
A (F A	U G T &	£ A Q A	

GLOSSARY

ALGORITHM: in the context of cryptography, a general set of procedures used to encrypt a message. The specifics of any particular encryption are established by the key.

CAESAR SHIFT: a cipher in which every letter in a message is replaced with a letter a certain number of places further along in the alphabet.

CIPHER: A method of hiding the meaning of a message by replacing the letters of the original with other letters. Unlike codes, ciphers do not take into account the meaning of the original words.

CIPHERTEXT: The text that results from applying a cipher to a given message.

CODE: A way to hide the meaning of a message by replacing words or phrases in the original with other words, phrases, or symbols that are contained in a set list.

CRYPTANALYSIS: The science of figuring out the plaintext message from the ciphertext, without knowledge of the specific way in which it was encrypted.

CRYPTOGRAPHY: The science of concealing the meaning of a message.

DECIPHER: To turn an enciphered message back into its original form.

ENCRYPTION: a term that encompasses encoding – turning a message into code – and enciphering – turning a message into cipher.

FREQUENCY ANALYSIS: the technique of comparing the frequency with which particular letters appear in a piece of ciphertext to the known frequencies in normal language.

HOMOPHONES: multiple substations that can replace a single letter in a cipher. For example, the letter 'a' could be replaced by several different letters or numbers, each of which are called homophones.

KEY: The instructions that specify the way a particular message will be encrypted, such as the arrangement of letters in the cipher alphabet.

NOMENCLATOR: A system that is part code, part cipher, which includes a list of names, words, and syllables like a code, plus a cipher alphabet.

PLAINTEXT: the text of a message before it is put into secret form.

POLYALPHABETIC CIPHER: a method for creating a cipher by using more than one replacement alphabet.

PRETTY GOOD PRIVACY (PGP): a computer encryption algorithm.

QUANTUM COMPUTER: a computer that would exploit the quantum mechanical nature of particles to manipulate information as quantum bits, or qubits. Whereas an ordinary bit has at any time a value of either 0 or 1, a qubit can also take on both values at once.

QUANTUM CRYPTOGRAPHY: A cryptographic system that uses the properties of quantum mechanics to ensure that evesdroppers are able to be detected.

RSA: The public key encryption method used in PGP, named after its developers – Ronald Rivest, Adi Shamir, and Leonard Adelman. Its security comes from the fact that it is computationally difficult to find the two prime factors of a given number.

STEGANOGRAPHY: The science of hiding the very existence of a secret message, rather than just obscuring its meaning.

SUBSTITUTION CIPHER: A system in which each letter in a message is replaced with another symbol.

TRANSPOSITION CIPHER: A system in which the letters in a message are rearranged within the message, but retain their identities.

INDEX

Page numbers in *italic* type refer to illustrations.

FURTHER READING

There are many detailed and specialist books available for those who would like to delve more deeply into the world of cryptology. We've listed a few of them below.

Annales des Mines. French mining journal detailing the life of Georges-Jean Painvin.

Bauer, F. L., *Decrypted Secrets*, Berlin: Springer, 2002.

Calvocoressi, Peter, *Top Secret Ultra*, London: Baldwin, 2001.

Carter, Frank, *The First Breaking of Enigma*, The Bletchley Park Trust Reports, No. 10, 1999

Deutsch, David, *The Fabric of Reality*, London: Penguin, 1997.

D'Imperio, M. E., *The Voynich Manuscript: An Elegant Enigma*, National Security Agency: 1978

Gallehawk, John, *Some Polish Contributions in the Second World War*, The Bletchley Park Trust Reports, No. 15, 1999

Kahn, David, *Seizing the Enigma*, London: Arrow Books, 1996.

Kahn, David, *The Code-Breakers*, New York: Scribner, 1996.

Levy, David, *Crypto*, New York: Penguin, 2000.

National Security Agency, *Masked Dispatches: Cryptograms and Cryptology in American History, 1775–1900*, National Security Agency: 2002

National Security Agency, *The Friedman Legacy: A Tribute to William and Elizabeth Friedman*, Sources in Cryptologic History Number 3, National Security Agency: 1992.

Newton, David E., *Encyclopedia of Cryptology*, Santa Barbara, CA: ABC-Clio, 1997.

Rivest, R., Shamir, A., and Adleman, L., 'A Method for Obtaining Digital Signatures and Public-Key Cryptosystems' in *Communications of the A.C.M.*, Vol. 21 (2), 1978, pp.120–126

Singh, Simon, *The Code Book*, London: 4th Estate, 1999.

Wrixon, Fred B., *Codes, Ciphers and other Cryptic and Clandestine Communication*, New York: Black Dog and Leventhal, 1998.

PICTURE CREDITS